'Tracey Thorn turns the tables on her teenage boredom and chips a jewel out of doing stuff – and not doing stuff – in suburbia. A meditation on mooching and moping, escaping and finding, mums and dads, love and ageing, which is reflective, warm and deeply touching'
Keggie Carew

'You could read a dense, meticulously researched history of post-war Britain, and end up understanding less about what it was like to be a young woman facing adulthood on the cusp of the 80s than you inhale so casually here'
Deborah Orr, *i*

'As an exploration of what it meant to grow up in the 1970s, *Another Planet* will resonate with people a long way from London's commuter belt'
Herald

'*Another Planet* is a wise and witty memoir of suburbia and how to escape it'
New Statesman America

'Thorn writes with considerable wit and poignancy, capturing the aspirations of the post-war generation – and the ennui of their children'
i

'There's so much to adore about musician and writer Tracey Thorn's love (and hate) letter to Brookman's Park, the Hertfordshire commuter town where she grew up . . . Hilariously and poignantly captured . . . *Another Planet* is sure to strike a chord with anyone who spent their adolescence yearning for the city's mean streets'
Red

Also by Tracey Thorn

Bedsit Disco Queen
Naked at the Albert Hall

Another Planet

'Beautiful . . . Made me catch my breath . . . Her language is
straightforward, chatty, easy-to-read. Musical'
Financial Times

'*Another Planet* made me yearn for a suburban childhood and a night
out dancing with Tracey Teen . . . Tender, funny
and unexpectedly dark'
Damian Barr

'Readers of Thorn's two previous memoirs will recognise the tone
of this book, with its beautifully clean style, careful
self-questioning and pervasive likability'
Guardian

'A thoughtful guide to the 70s as [Thorn] muses
on her teenage years in rural Hertfordshire'
Daily Mail

'I loved it. Thorn is the rarest of things: a singer whose phrasing
is as good on the page as it is through a microphone'
John Niven

'[Thorn's] resolute honesty, quietly modest manner, and the simple
eloquence of her writing has seen her stand out among other artists
who have made comparable career leaps'

Another Planet

A TEENAGER IN SUBURBIA

TRACEY THORN

CANONGATE

This paperback edition published in 2020 by Canongate Books

First published in Great Britain, the USA and Canada in 2019
by Canongate Books Ltd, 14 High Street, Edinburgh EH1 1TE

Distributed in the USA by Publishers Group West
and in Canada by Publishers Group Canada

canongate.co.uk

1

For permission credits please see p. 213

British Library Cataloguing-in-Publication Data
A catalogue record for this book is available on
request from the British Library

ISBN 978 1 78689 258 4

Typeset in Garamond MT Std by
Palimpsest Book Production Ltd, Falkirk, Stirlingshire

Printed and bound in Great Britain by Clays Ltd, Elcograf S.p.A.

For Debbie and Keith
And in memory of Audrey and Dennis
With love

PREFACE

'You look as if you wished the place in Hell,'
My friend said, 'judging from your face.' 'Oh well,
I suppose it's not the place's fault,' I said.
'Nothing, like something, happens anywhere.'
          (Philip Larkin: 'I Remember, I Remember')

When I try to summon up the past – when I want to remember what really happened, instead of what I think happened, and what I really felt, instead of what I'd like to think I felt, and what I really did, instead of what I say I did – I look at my diaries. They never fail to shock me with all the things they say, and all the things they don't. Going right back to the start, I try to picture myself on the day I first decided to keep a diary: 29 December 1975, when I was thirteen years old. I must have been given it as a Christmas present, and although it was for the year 1976, its first few pages invited entries for the end of the previous year. So I began as the old year ended, just before it turned to face the new.

I would have settled down with a pen, riffled through

1

the year's worth of blank, empty pages before breaking it open at the very start, and then:

29 December 1975 – *'Went to St Albans with Debbie. Got a belt. Could not get a jumper or skirt.'*

That's it, that's all she wrote. No starting with a bang, no announcing herself to the world, or to a future reader, no declaration of intent. Nothing along the lines of 'Dear Diary, draw closer and listen to what I have to say. Here I am; this is me; let me tell you the story of my life.' Not even the guileless enthusiasm of a thirteen-year-old self-introduction – 'Hello, I'm Tracey and this is my diary.' Instead, I draw a circle and leave it empty, my eye caught by an absence. And it wasn't an aberration; I carried on in that style for years, making countless entries about not buying things, not going to the disco, not going to school, a piano lesson being cancelled, the school coach not arriving. It's a life described by what's missing, and what fails to happen.

My second-ever entry is just as banal:

30 December – *'Went to Welwyn with Liz. Didn't get anything except a bag of Kentucky chips.'*

Was it me or was it my surroundings? Was it just that I was the dullest child in existence, noticing nothing, experiencing nothing, thinking nothing, or was it at least in part an embodiment of something in the air, something vague and undefined? Even when I write about it now, I realise that the time and place in which I grew up, 1970s suburbia, is easier to define by saying what it wasn't than what it was. Brookmans Park was a village but not a village. Rural but not rural. A stop on the line, a space in between two landscapes that are both more highly rated – the city, and the countryside. A contingent, liminal, border territory. In-betweenland.

1 January 1977 – *'Went to Welwyn with Mum and Dad to get some boots but couldn't get any.'*

8 January – *'Liz and I went to Potters Bar in the afternoon to try to get her ears pierced, but she couldn't.'*

Anywhere with a tube station, however 'end of the line' that stop may be, still feels to me like part of London, physically linked by the tunnels and rails. Things would still happen there. But beyond the reach of the Underground lies a different and less certain terrain. Where things might not happen at all. Where you might continually try but continually fail, in endless small endeavours.

19 January 1979 – *'Deb and I went to St Albans. Tried to get some black trousers but couldn't find any nice ones.'*

17 March – *'Tried to go to the library but it was shut.'*

When I came to write a song about the place, 'Oxford Street', I fell back into this habit of describing by subtraction, stating what wasn't there – 'Where I grew up there were no factories' – and only then going on to admit that 'there was a school and shops, and some fields and trees'. But although there were fields, there was no agricultural life. No one worked as a farmer. All the men got on the train every morning with a briefcase to go up to town. Nature writers would have found little there to describe; it was not a place of shepherds, or hawks. There was no real scenery – no hills, or lakes, nothing in the way of a view.

Here I am again, talking about what it is not. What is it about the place that it demands to be written about in such an equivocal way? I rebelled as a teen and so have often felt there was a clean break between my past and my future – that I abandoned the old me and invented a new one, casting off the time and place I came from. But as I get older, I sense its presence inside me. I think I want to reconnect with the self I left behind. It's partly that common impulse of curiosity – which informs a TV programme like *Who Do You Think You Are?* or a song like 'Where Do You Go To My Lovely'. I want to look inside my head and remember just where I came from. Because I can't quite believe it was as lacking as my diary suggests.

Like the negative of a photo, it's as if the Technicolor version of life were happening elsewhere, full of events and successes, dreams and achievements. Meanwhile, whenever I tried to sum up the place where I lived and the life I was living, I would write over and over again: this didn't happen, that didn't happen. It's neither one thing nor another, and I'm neither here nor there.

2016

I'm on a train back to my childhood, as though it still exists, as tangible and re-visitable as the place I left behind. Although it feels a hundred years ago and a thousand miles away, it is – nonetheless – actually only fifty-three minutes on the train, with one change, from what is now my nearest station, Finchley Road & Frognal. The last time I took this train was probably thirty years ago. I wouldn't have had a phone in my bag. No one would. I wouldn't have had a child, but I would still have had both parents. I would have been on my way to see them.

The London Overground train is packed, standing room only and air-conditioned to iciness, yet it still has that city buzz which is a kind of warmth, everyone jostling prams and backpacks and suitcases, and it's busy in that city way, everyone heads down or engrossed in something, to try to create a tiny private space. Through Hampstead Heath and Gospel Oak, to Kentish Town West, which would have been my mum's nearest stop when she was growing up in London. Between here and Camden Road there are buildings going up beside the line, cranes in the sky everywhere you look, London still growing and still filling in every gap. At Highbury & Islington I head to the platform for trains heading north, and the crowd thins out. By the time I am waiting for the train to Welwyn Garden City, there are only five people left, while at the far end a man whistles tunelessly and eerily, the notes fading away into the tunnel.

On the train, discarded copies of the *Metro* litter the seats, and we pull out of the station to a close-up view of the Emirates Stadium. Then Drayton Park, and a brand-new-looking, blue-clad block of flats, curved like a liner, and another clad in chequered tiles – blue and grey, green and grey, orange and grey. At Finsbury Park there is construction going on, orange-clad highly visible workmen loiter beside pile drivers. This would have been Dad's nearest stop when he was growing up in London. The scenery is still an urban blur of Victorian terraced houses backing on to the line, window boxes and washing, depots and warehouses, graffiti sprayed on the blackened brick-work. At Harringay, a builders' yard, 'cement and plasterboard', industrial grey corrugated-iron sheds, while at Hornsey, the tall gold dome of the London Islamic Cultural Society and Mosque is visible from the station. Up on a hill to the left, Alexandra Palace, where Dad roller-skated as a child, sits in splendour, and at the station the train begins to empty out. What looks like a huge abandoned factory is covered in hard-edged, geometric graffiti, and then there's a long tunnel, and an industrial estate, planks and pallets, and piles and piles of bricks.

I've brought a sandwich with me to eat on the train, as if I imagine there won't be any food to be had this far north of the city, as if I'm going off exploring into the wilds. Although, on the other hand, it is also quite suburban of me to have brought a sandwich. A train picnic for a journey lasting fifty-three minutes. At New Southgate there's a change of style, the houses no longer Victorian or Edwardian, but more like 1960s or '70s. Low blocks of flats and a car park, a line of pine trees, and then another long tunnel, followed by more greenery, more trees beside the line, tags on concrete amid the leaves.

Oakleigh Park is the first stop outside the London post-code, and it merges into New Barnet, modern semi-detached housing and flats, small gardens with washing lines, sheds and plastic greenhouses, the kind of suburbia that is true urban sprawl, the shallow waters of the city. The train is almost empty, which gives me the creeps, increasing the feeling that I'm leaving behind the bustle and safety of the crowd. It gets quieter and quieter, although inside my head the noise seems to be getting louder, competing thoughts crowding in, a faint sound in the background that might be a scream, and a voice saying quite insistently, 'Am I really doing this? Am I really going there?' More fields and trees appear, I think I'm seeing the actual Green Belt before my eyes. It's another reason for this journey, for this whole project, my realisation that the kind of suburbia I grew up in is endlessly fascinating to me. I think of John Updike's line about trying in his writing to give 'the mundane its beautiful due', and I've always liked that notion of turning the gaze upon the commonplace, or the overlooked. There's nothing especially beautiful about where I came from, and yet its role in my life is huge, and there's something inherently respectful, isn't there, about properly looking at a place, paying it the compliment of being worthy of attention?

Another tunnel, then Hadley Wood, hawthorn in blossom, buddleia heavy with last year's rusty, dead flower heads. A huge willow tree, brambles and rosebay willow herb. Open countryside, gently hilly fields separated by hedgerows, and then another tunnel. All these tunnels! I'd never noticed them before, was never paying any attention, and yet here they've been, ever since the railway had to find a way through the chalky hills surrounding the London Basin.

Nearly there now. Potters Bar. A car park, a Sainsbury's, a view of the high street shops, and very definitely suburban. We're not in London any more, Toto. Silver birches, a Union Jack flying, the golf course on the right, and the car park where, years after I'd left, and playing no part in my story except for the way it slightly haunts me, a murder took place. A field full of solar panels to the left, and then here we are, houses nestling in the gentle green: Brookmans Park.

Brookmans Park, in the county of Hertfordshire, sits in a sea of green just off the coast of London. Not a river, but a railway runs through it, and is the reason for its existence. The station – opened by the London and North Eastern Railway (LNER) on 19 July 1926 – is located fourteen miles north of Kings Cross on the East Coast Main Line, making it the perfect spot for a commuter village, which duly developed from the 1930s onwards. I was born there, in the front bedroom of our house, in 1962 and spent my childhood believing that I lived in a village in the countryside. I rarely ventured further than the primary school round the corner, or the shops that clustered round the village green, perhaps stopping to give a sugar lump to the horse in the pasture near the station. There were three directions out of the village and whichever one you took, you'd soon be driving past fields.

There was a livery stable called Raybrook Farm, where I would go with my friend Liz who'd ride a pony, while I hung around, not wanting to ride a pony. Next to the primary school was Peplins Wood, where we took nature walks, carrying laminated sheets of facts about squirrels and oak trees, native plants and beetles, an only slightly more formalised version of filling in an I-Spy book. We'd collect tadpoles in the spring, and make an excursion to see the bluebells, a vivid carpet the colour of a child's eyes, which seemed to pull the sky down into the woods. Although when we played in the woods in the summer holidays, the air of innocence was dispelled as we built dens and formed gangs, boys vs girls, and menace hung in the air. Later on when I read *Lord of the Flies*, and watched *Blue Remembered Hills*, I had an inkling of what had seemed so namelessly frightening.

My friends' houses backed on to fields, and one summer evening, aged about eight, I got lost in the tall wheat with Sandra. By the time I'd reached home, late and in trouble, my eyes were streaming and bloodshot with hayfever. I'd been scared. The meadows had seemed suddenly alien and pathless, with no obvious route through them. I'd feared being lost, being late, being followed; that darkness would fall and trap us there, in the chill that falls on an English field at dusk, even at the end of a warm day.

At Gobions Wood – the remnants of an old estate, now a public park – Dad and my brother Keith would go fishing beside the lake at 5 a.m., next to other men and their sons, dressed in olive green, silent in the dawn with flasks of tea. The lake dried out in the heatwave summer of 1976 and would freeze over in winter, daring us to skate on it in defiance of the Public Information films we watched at school. There was a playground there, where teenagers hung out on the swings, or lounged on the heavy wooden roundabout that needed the heft of two people to get moving. But it was less a place to play, more a place to smoke.

In autumn crab apples lay squashed on the pavement, and in the damp air hung the smell of a bonfire: Mum at the back of the garden burning leaves and rubbish in a metal incinerator; Dad gathering sharp Cox's Orange Pippin apples and wrapping them in newspaper. Winter brought snow, and as late as Easter one year enough fell that we made an igloo in the garden, using sheets of glassy ice from the pond to form a skylight roof, like a modern Scandi hotel. Summer was spent in the garden, each of us given a patch to plant, marked out with pebbles and sea shells, filled with marigolds and snapdragons. We'd open up furry lupin seed heads to find the tiny pearls within, and earn pocket money by weeding out the chickweed and speedwell.

But most of what we did with nature was kill it: gathering rose petals to make perfume in a jam jar, wondering why after only five minutes it would settle into a stagnant stinky pond, or putting caterpillars into a shoe box with leaves, and holes poked in the lid, and wondering why they'd shrivel and die within a day or two. We'd pop the buds on the fuchsia despite Dad telling us it would kill the flowers. Our garden backed onto that of the Griffin family, with an old oak tree between us, beneath which they kept a rabbit in a hutch. We looked after it one year while they were on holiday, and rats broke in. When we went to feed and give it water, we found it dead in the cage. Blood on the white fur.

I took part every year in the fête at the primary school, which was called Village Day. The usual bric-a-brac and cake stalls, tombola and coconut shy, sat alongside a maypole, around which I learned to dance. What could be more rural, more ancient and traditional than that? It sounds authentic and historical, but like everything else, Village Day was new, started by the primary school head-master in order to raise money to build the swimming pool in the late 1950s. We would freeze there in summer, in armbands and skirted costumes, kicking up and down with white polystyrene floats. I discovered recently that the pool has since been filled in.

Nearby there were places with REAL history. St Albans, where I started going in my teens, had Roman ruins. An abbey. Georgian and Victorian houses. Private schools, one each for girls and boys. A medieval clock tower, beneath which we would meet in order to go and drink in the medieval pub, The Boot. In Hatfield was Hatfield House, dating from 1611 and sitting near the remains of an even earlier royal palace, childhood home of Elizabeth I. There are Grade II-listed seventeenth-century houses in Old

Hatfield, but also nearby, Grade II-listed Modernist houses. Buildings that were properly old, or properly new.

Brookmans Park, in contrast, had no history at all, it was a bland, characterless development of little boxes that sprang up overnight somehow, in a void. Nothing was here before it was built; it was a stage set dropped onto an empty landscape. Or so I thought until I started looking. In fact, like all land in England, it had belonged to someone, for a long time the same family, the Gaussens, who owned the Brookmans estate. A mansion, with its park and fields and woods, was bought in 1786 by Peter Gaussen, Governor of the Bank of England, for £16,000, and his family would live there for the next 135 years.

In 1891 the manor house was destroyed by fire while the owner was cruising on his yacht, and the house was never rebuilt, the family instead converting the stable block into their home. In 1906 the estate was handed on to daughter Emilia and her husband, Hubert Ponsonby Loftus Tottenham. Financial difficulties followed, loans and mortgages, the downward trajectory of landowning families, and after 1914 parts of the estate began to be sold off, the family living in reduced scale in their converted stable. The end came in 1923 when 969 acres of their land was bought by a syndicate of developers, who formed a company, Brookmans Park (Hatfield) Ltd, in order to construct a commuter village.

Originally the plan was for a garden city, along the lines of Welwyn Garden City, the second garden city in England, which was founded in 1920 only five miles away. There would have been a town square, and a much bigger, more

13

urban development, but the scheme was gradually scaled down. After the railway station opened in July 1926, building began. Right from the start there were disputes about the necessity of what we'd call affordable housing, but which were then referred to as 'workmen's cottages'. In 1928 the only subsidised houses were built – more were planned, but never materialised, as the developers claimed they couldn't afford to build properties that would command a lower rent. Already much of the housing was aspirational rather than affordable, and some existing homeowners objected to the building of bungalows – the dispute was settled when it was agreed to build a 'better class of bungalow'.

A better class of bungalow.

2016

I step off the train, up and over the footbridge, feeling a swerve of vertigo on the open-tread steps, remembering how my mum had real trouble going up and down them, thrown off balance by the sight of the drop. There's a view of sharp, fresh green all around, oak trees by the road bridge, the footpath already fuzzy with goose grass. A sign reads, 'To the Shops and the Golf Course', and another, reassuringly, 'CCTV is looking after you here'. There are sixteen new luxury homes being built right next to the station, a small development that must have broken through the red tape of planning and the outrage of local opposition. The battles of the Green Belt are still being fought here: debate rages about new housing proposals, many residents wanting to stop Brookmans Park itself expanding, and thus filling in the green space between it and London. It's a hot local topic.

Down from the station, the village shops stand exactly as they did, no change in style or size, only in the goods they sell or services they provide. Cutting It Fine, the hair salon, sits next to a wine seller that was a long-established off-licence, then a new osteopath practice and a takeaway

15

offering kebabs/burgers/pizza. A dry cleaner's, a tea room, and Methi Indian Cuisine, which used to be the wool shop. One of FOUR estate agents, one of SIX beauty salons, followed by Raj Indian Cuisine, and the Wing Wah Garden, which opened in 1977. The first place offering 'foreign' food, it brought a literal taste of the outside world and exposed all our limitations and prejudices. A local family said they'd move if a Chinese takeaway opened, which gave rise to a truly memorable row at my house, when my mum argued that it wasn't just people in Brookmans Park who thought like that, to which I replied, 'No, Brookmans Park doesn't have a monopoly on racism!' I was proud of my use of the word monopoly, which I'd only just learned, and expected cheers, but instead it provoked fury and then silence. I hear myself saying it now and I sound a bit smug. A bit teenage. But I still think I was right.

I turn left at the fishmonger, and pass a small green-grocer (closed on Thursdays), another hair studio, and a dental practice where the garage used to be. The chemist is where the chemist always used to be, and next to it a Co-op where the supermarket always used to be, and where I had my first Saturday job. Two more estate agents, the Beauty in the Park salon, Groomers on the Green (dogs) in the lovely curved 1930s shopfront that was a green-grocer/pet shop. I'm delighted to see that the library is still here and still open, and the bakery is still a bakery, and the newsagent is still a newsagent, and the toyshop is still a toyshop, and the butcher's is still a butcher's, and the hairdresser's is still a hairdresser's, although now called a hair boutique. Peering through the window, I see the half-moon tables, and curly backed chairs, and overhead driers, unchanged since the 1970s.

The DIY store is another Chinese restaurant. Amazing that the population has survived the introduction of no less than four places selling 'foreign' food. You might almost think people turned out to like it after all. Bringing us bang up to date, there is Body in Balance, specialising in sorting out back pain, and finally, in place of the bank, an Organic Dry Cleaner's. The same number of shops as there ever were, thirty-nine, and so many still the same.

As I walk around, I'm struck by how well the place seems to be doing. There is no atmosphere of rural decline. The closing of village shops and pubs, and local schools, and libraries, and the dwindling of rural bus and train services – Brookmans Park seems to have been spared most of this, in contrast to what we might call the 'real' countryside, which in many areas has suffered blight and neglect. There is money here, and the village has proved itself to be impervious to both change and decline. Some of the shops, and pavements and road surfaces, look a bit shabby, a bit in need of updating, but that's the worst you could say. I walk up to look at the church, where the sound of fast trains going through is loud. Solar panels on a detached house.

1976

A pocket-sized diary with a red leather cover, measuring 4 × 3 inches. A week to two pages, it allowed enough room for three short sentences per day. On the front is the word 'Haig' and inside, beside a picture of two bottles, the words, 'Haig – Britain's Largest Selling Scotch Whisky. Don't Be Vague Ask For Haig'. There follow three or four pages of metric imperial conversion tables, the year's bank holidays, and then a 'Wine Chart', the years from 1948 to 1973 rated as a score of 0–7 for Claret, Red Burgundy, White Burgundy, Sauternes, Champagne and Port. And just to remind me where I didn't live, a tube map, and then a map of the West End, detailing for me the area between the Thames and Oxford Street, where I hardly ever went.

It begins just before the old year ended, with those entries from December 1975, about being unable to get a jumper or a skirt, buying nothing except a bag of chips, although the year ended on a high, with this triumphant entry for New Year's Eve: '*Liz came over in the morning, and I bought some things from the chemist.*'

I was thirteen years old, life was slow and even, and very little happened, over and over again. '*Deb and I went* to *St Albans, Hatfield, Potters Bar and Barnet!! Got nothing except a Peanuts writing pad.' 'Tried to phone Deb but no answer.'* My emotional range was restricted to my feelings about David Essex, nothing and no one else seeming to rouse any passion in me; the films *That'll be the Day* and *Stardust* were described in detail, on a page decorated with love hearts, and the words 'sob sob' repeated. Those films tell the tale of a rock star's rise to glory and his descent into drug-addled failure, and I watched wide-eyed and open-mouthed, entranced by the beauty and the glamour of it all.

1976 began with snow, and I was off school with a cold. '*I went to Raybrook Farm,*' and there was '*a heron in the garden. It tried to eat the goldfish.*' Because of the limited local shops, I bought things from Mum's catalogue, and listed every tiny, insignificant purchase made when I did leave the house, '*Went to Welwyn, got a face pack.*' To pass the time, like everyone else I watched a lot of telly, and the same telly as everyone else. Limited by three channels, we were bonded by watching and sharing the same few programmes, all of which I listed in my diary: *Supersonic, Upstairs Downstairs, Crossroads* and *Candid Camera . . . The Waltons, Little House on the Prairie, McCloud, New Faces* and *Ellery Queen . . . Who Do You Do?, Columbo, Survivors, Porridge* and *Monty Python's Flying Circus . . . Call My Bluff, Bionic Man, New Avengers, Starsky & Hutch, Superstars* and *Kojak . . . The Six Million Dollar Man, Hawaii Five-O.* There'd be a film on Saturday night – *From Russia with Love, South Pacific, I'm All Right Jack . . . Guess Who's Coming to Dinner, Singin' in the Rain, The Nutty Professor.*

Most of all I loved the comedy: *The Dave Allen Show,*

Fawlty Towers, *Morecambe and Wise*, *Tomkinson's Schooldays* and *The Good Life*, which, of course, was a satire about suburbia, the idealistic Goods trying to exchange their suburban life for a more rural, meaningful one. It was funny, but also full of contemporary ideas about escaping the rat race, getting back to a utopian notion of self-sufficiency, living off the land. Tom Good suggested there was more value to this kind of life than could be found in modern Surbiton, though Margo and Jerry were there to provide the counterpoint, laughing at him and being laughed at in their turn. The kind of street they lived in, the kind of gardens they had, looked familiar to me, although I could see that my parents weren't much like the Goods – who were dungaree-wearing semi-hippies, unconventional and liberal – but were in fact more like Margo and Jerry: conservative, aspirational, repressed. The atmosphere in the Goods house was relaxed and cheerful, but next door, Margo was uptight, with no sense of humour, while Gerry was cowardly and trapped. And it wasn't hard to see that they were the villains, while the Goods were the good guys. That worried me a bit.

If TV programmes were limited, so was our access to music. I bought the David Essex single 'Rock On' from a friend, and on another day, *'Deb and I bought batteries for the tape recorder. It's really good. Taped Neil Sedaka, Pluto and Four Seasons.'* We'd never heard anyone say that home-taping was killing music. It wouldn't have meant anything to us. Home-taping was bringing some music into our house, and was one of the few ways we could do so, along with the radio, and Dial-a-Disc, where you'd sit at the phone table in the hall and dial a certain number in order to listen to a tinny recording of the current number seven single.

Every weekday I listed my school lessons, wasting pages and pages on what was just my timetable – *'English, maths, double cookery, hockey, double German, music, double science, Swimming!!'*

And here's what a weekend looked like for a thirteen-year-old in 1976:

Saturday – *'Liz and I went to Welwyn today. Got a face pack and a hideaway stick thingy. Went to Liz's in the afternoon. Had a bath and washed hair. Saw some Winter Olympics. Bed at 10.30.'*

Sunday – *'Did housework in morning and got 65p. Had roast lamb for din dins. Ordered a waistcoat from Freemans. Also a floor cushion. Saw M*A*S*H. Bed at 9.30.'*

Or the following weekend:

Saturday – *'Got a letter from Anne. Went to Hatfield. Got earrings and mascara. Deb went to a disco. Liz stayed the night. Saw* Upstairs Downstairs *in bed.'*

Sunday – *'Got up at 11. Went to shops. Liz stayed for dinner. Roast lamb, etc. Liz went home at 3.30. Tidied room. Wardrobe too. Listened to the charts. Bed at 9.'*

The diary is incredibly boring, and yet cheerful – there are no confessions of anything, just endless meals, lessons, bedtimes and shopping trips. A few pages where I changed

21

writing style or pen colour, and then an entry – *'Isn't this diary getting messy – sorry!!'* – which begs the question, who was I apologising to? Who was all this for? Who is ANY diary for? Such a catalogue of the humdrum, it would eventually mutate into a seething stew of truth and lies, revelation and concealment. In later years I would lie about what I was feeling, and one memorable day, even leave a page entirely blank, unable or unwilling to find words for what had happened.

Part of the problem was that I wasn't convinced my diary was private, and had every reason to suspect that my mum would read it whenever possible. One day she'd made a casual remark about regretting having had kids, and I wrote a dramatic letter to a friend saying that this revelation had made me consider suicide, which wasn't true in any real sense at all, but Mum found the unsealed letter on my bed, read it and confronted me. So I didn't confide entirely to my diary, as I couldn't be sure who I was telling – although a psychologist might have something to say about all of this. The unsealed letter, for instance. Why did I leave it like that, lying on my bed? Why didn't I hide my diary properly? Why was I sometimes honest and sometimes not? You might think I was telling her certain things, hiding others. Testing limits. Sounding out a response.

In my 1970s commuter village, I never heard the word 'class' used, and yet we all knew what it was, and everyone knew where they stood in the pecking order. Even for such a tiny place, there was a right and a wrong end of town. No one was truly posh because they hadn't been there long enough, and if being upper-class is a matter of history, ancestry and inheritance – property that's been passed down, land that has been owned for generations – then no one in Brookmans Park could claim that. There were bigger houses, but they were all as new as each other, and even the detached ones with gravel drives and wide gardens looked unmistakably suburban.

If there was no upper class, there was no real working class either – there were no factories, no mines, no farms, no heavy industry. But this is not to say there was no hierarchy, and no looking down on people. Looking down on people was a favourite hobby, and the word used was 'common'. My mum called people common, even though when she spoke on the phone to her own mother her accent would slip a few notches, back to where it originated in a Kentish Town terrace.

In our house, being common seemed to be both about class and about other things. My friend S's mum dyed her hair bright yellow and wore a mini dress with a chain belt, and she was common. Her husband had a grown-out duck's-arse hairdo and wore chunky jewellery, and he was common too. Swearing was common, too much make-up was common, sex was common. The word described vulgarity as much as class, and a terror of being infected by that vulgarity. People who were common were not trying hard enough.

When I left home, and met more worldly middle-class people, I realised that being called Tracey, and saying lounge and serviette and settee, meant that, whatever my mum thought, I may as well have had the word COMMON branded on my forehead. Throughout the 1980s the names 'Sharon' and 'Tracey' were the ubiquitous markers of work-ing-class womanhood. In their choice of my name, my parents had blundered horribly, any Sharons and Traceys being the 'chavs' or Essex girls of their day. And yet what was I really? I wasn't a chav, despite my name, and yet I felt different from people I met at university, who were posher, or urban, or rural. And it wasn't easy to be defiant and proud about the difference. For I wasn't working class. I was suburban; a bit semi-detached. Almost a class of its own. Privileged in many ways, yes, but also sometimes scorned.

Along with the dislike of vulgarity, went a distrust of what was called 'showing off'. Particularly disagreeable in children, it was not welcomed in adults either, and included any kind of assertiveness, individualism, eccentricity. What should be aimed for was anonymity, not drawing attention to yourself, in the hope that such quietness would be quietly acknowledged and rewarded. These were properly suburban values. Abstinence and piety defined the suburb – Robert Gaussen, the owner of the original Brookmans estate, was a supporter of the temperance movement in the mid-nineteenth century, and the Band of Hope would march from the church to the mansion for tea in a marquee – in sharp contrast to the sinful city, which was still regarded when I was a teenager as a place full of sex and drugs and rock and roll.

Being in a band was probably showing off, I think now. I did a little bit of drama as a child, and acted in a primary school play, but it was all at a low enough level to be simply child-like and charming. Buying a guitar later on, and starting to sing, was much more demonstrative and self-aggrandising, and perhaps it's no wonder that I always had trouble with summoning up the required self-confidence and assertiveness. Always in the back of my head was a voice telling me to stop showing off. Don't make a spectacle. Put that drink down. Shhhh.

But I wonder sometimes, what difference does it make growing up in an environment where you are not told to be quiet and stop showing off? It's often written that Bjork grew up on a commune, moving there with her activist mother after her parents split up. Bjork herself has said, in an interview on a French fan website (bjork.fr) 'I was the only child there, and they all had long hair . . . If I thought I had something to say, people would listen to me. And people would play me records that they were listening to, and explain them to me.' At the age of six she was studying piano and flute at school, and after singing on Iceland's only radio station, she was offered a recording contract and released her first album, aged twelve.

I've seen footage of her performing onstage with her band Tappi Tikarrass, still aged only seventeen, and before forming the Sugarcubes, but already full of energy, confidence and style. An untrammelled performer, expressive, vivid, not afraid to be loud. And I think – is that what growing up in that environment does, where you are listened to and records are played to you? Is it that which liberated her as an artist, or was it in her anyway? Would she have been that person if she'd grown up in Surbiton?

J.G. Ballard was famous for living in suburbia most of his life, but was considered unusual as an artist for doing so. He lived in a 1930s semi in Shepperton for decades, in a street filled with houses called 'Laurel View' and 'Ivy Dene', and claimed that he valued the insight it afforded him into middle-class English life. But the continuing surprise at Ballard's decision to remain in suburbia reveals how we can't quite believe in it as an appropriate setting for anyone creative. Artists are meant to cluster together in the city or seek complete isolation. The properly rural – a croft in the Orkneys, a cottage on a hillside – is gritty in its own green way, while the properly urban – a loft, a garret – is avant-garde and exciting. Those in between, who live in clusters of modest homes, bigger than villages but smaller than towns, are looked down upon. We don't like to admit to coming from suburbia. It's a place you're supposed to want to run away from.

And yet it constantly gives birth to people who stretch and break these constraints. David Bowie may have been born in Brixton, but when he was seven his family moved to Bromley in Kent. An old market town since the twelfth century, it had been swallowed up by London's expansion in the twentieth century, and became an example of that type of suburb. Only nine miles from Charing Cross and part of Greater London, which was more townie than where I grew up and yet still not truly metropolitan – separate from the centre yet close enough for those who lived there to have their noses pressed up against the glass of London's windows.

From that suburban setting sprang his iconoclasm, his rule-breaking, perhaps proving that commonly held belief that growing up in a conservative environment is inspiring, giving the artistic type something to kick against, a reason to rebel. Following in Bowie's footsteps in the mid-'70s were a group of his fans who became known as 'the Bromley Contingent', and who are often thought of as the first true punks. Made up of characters like Siouxsie Sioux, Steve Severin, Billy Idol, Jordan, Soo Catwoman, Debbie Juvenile and Tracie O'Keefe, they were the ones who confronted Bill Grundy with the Sex Pistols on TV in 1976, and who were arrested after the famous Malcolm McLaren-organised boat trip down the Thames during the Queen's Silver Jubilee celebrations. They were the ones who worked in Seditionaries, and whose pictures appeared in the press. I try to imagine them now, setting out for an evening in town, first having to leave their homes in those quiet, conventional streets. Did they get on the bus dressed like that? With their dramatic cat's-eye make-up, hair sculpted into spikes and wings, wearing dog collars and fishnets, Siouxsie black-lipsticked and bare-breasted? It would have taken guts to walk around Soho looking like that, but Bromley?

In Jon Savage's *England's Dreaming*, Siouxsie is quoted describing the place. 'I hated Bromley. I thought it was small and narrow-minded. There was this trendy wine bar called Pips, and I got Berlin to wear this dog-collar, and I walked in with Berlin following me, and people's jaws just hit the tables. I walked in and ordered a bowl of water for him, I got the bowl of water for my dog. People were scared!' Picture it. Going out for the evening, down to the trendy wine bar. Leaving the house, closing the front door behind you, stilettos clacking on the paved path, lifting the latch on a gate. Setting out into the suburban street, shutting the suburban gate of the suburban garden.

Those gardens were all the same, and ours was typical – a small front lawn, surrounded by flowerbeds full of peach and yellow roses, separated from the pavement by a low, crenellated brick wall, that little hint of the Englishman's castle. Our back garden was long and narrow, mostly lawn, and was where we played badminton, or put up a tent in the summer, as if the actual outdoors was too much. We'd sit sweating inside it, drinking orange squash and getting hayfever from the cut grass. Next door, Gladys grew flowers for the horticultural show – huge, overblown dahlias, bright and velvety, propped up with canes – and given that she was also chair of the local horticultural society, there was some grumbling when she won every cup every year.

Mum said that Dad gardened like the accountant he was, with everything in neat rows. That sounds rather cutting, but is not as vicious as the comment I once heard, that a neighbour was 'the kind of person who has too many annuals in the front garden'. Like everything else in this country, gardens reveal your class. There's a posh English style: shrubby perennials, plants that need staking, and which climb and tumble over canes and pea-sticks, sprawling and spreading with the untidy opulence of the shabby chic country house interior. The plants are the equivalent of worn rugs and inherited furniture, ideally set off by mossy statuary, lichen-encrusted stone urns and terracotta pots. Nowadays there's a new urban minimalist vernacular too – steel planters, bamboo, wooden screens, rectangular pools, pebbles – a low-maintenance, faux-Japanese style.

But our garden was a typical example of mid-twentieth-century suburban taste. Not terracotta but practical plastic containers, half-barrels and hanging baskets; a kidney-shaped goldfish pond; a small row of two-foot-high conifers in a bed outside the kitchen window; a whirligig clothes drier on a crazy-paving patio; a waist-high chain link fence between us and next door. Valuing tidiness above naturalness, Dad would mow the lawn as soon as daisies flourished, and then, as Mum pointed out, he would plant things in neat rows. And not necessarily the 'right' things. For plants can also be U and non-U. Peonies are quite posh, marigolds not. Wisteria posh, Busy Lizzies not. Alchemilla Mollis? Yes. Pampas Grass? Definitely no. Hostas not rockeries. Clematis not conifers. We loved our garden, but in these terms it was all wrong. Common, and too full of annuals. Who knew.

1976

The diary continued, comfortingly routine and uneventful.

20 February 1976 – *'Went to St Albans and Hatfield. Got jeans in Dimple, £8.75, and a waistcoat in Tamla.'*

6 March – *'Did paper round Bluebridge Rd.'*

8 March – *'Went to Brent Cross after school. It's lovely!! All indoors. Got a shirt, scarf and a necklace.'* This would have been my first trip there, as it had only just opened.

27 March – *'Went to a disco in New Barnet. Cost 35p. It was good. Went with Liz, and Deb and the mob.'*

29 March – *'Liz's birthday. Got her some Aqua Manda talc and perfume. Went down the town after school with Deb. Didn't get anything. Bed at 9.'*

1 April – *'In registration we hid from Miss M and we turned all our room around for Mrs Evans. Deb put a notice on me*

– I AM A FOOL. Meanie. Bed at 9. Nannie and Grandad came.'

3 April – *'Dad lost Katy over the woods!! Found her though. (Phew!!) Got some jeans. Watched the Euro Song Contest. WE WON!! Hooray. Bed at 11.'*

I would describe what was in my packed lunch, *'cheese sarnies today'*, *'salmon paste rolls'*, and list the meals I made at school, all of them straight from a 1970s magazine. *'Made hot Swiss trifle in cookery . . . Did a salad in cookery . . . flaky pastry . . . sausage rolls . . . chicken vol au vents . . . Swiss roll . . . bread dough . . . pizza . . . a chocolate log'.*

In the spring I went to visit my friend Deborah, who had moved to Derby.

15 April – *'Went for a walk. In the afternoon we went to see* Jaws. *YEEUUCCHH!! It was REALLY GRUESOME. Got home at about 5.15. Watched* TOTP, Are You Being Served? *and* The Burke Special. *Bed at 9.30.'*

And then there's what I didn't say. After seeing *Jaws* I woke at 1.30 a.m., feeling sick and terrified. Sitting up in bed, staring bleakly into the dark, thinking about the black water, that tug from below, the body in the dunes, that rolling head, or was it just a skull? I wasn't looking by then. My mind was full of death and mutilation and horror. It was so vivid, such a formative experience, that I remember it clearly, and yet in the diary there was no room for such feelings. Deborah's Dad had come to comfort me as I was retching in the bathroom. 'Oh dear,' he said gently, '*Jaws*-type stomach?' 'NO!' I said, appalled that he'd think I was scared of a silly film. 'No, I must have eaten something. I just feel sick.' He wasn't fooled, but he didn't push me on it, or tease me, just sympathised. I couldn't admit being scared to him, or to my diary. If you didn't talk about things, they weren't happening. I was only thirteen. but I'd already learned the code.

Next day, '*We all went for a drive and had a drink in a pub! TUT TUT!! Bed about 10.*' That 'TUT TUT' was something I would often write to myself, sometimes about a late bedtime, sometimes about not doing homework – this time about having an underage drink. Was I judging myself? Or slightly bragging? Oooh, you naughty girl.

18 May – '*Did high jump at school, I could only do 1.15m TUT TUT.*'

19 May – '*Bed at half past 10 TUT TUT.*' Such mundanity, and then I didn't properly describe the things that did happen, like the first time I got off with a boy. It's there, but it's so brief you could miss it if you didn't know it was a first snog. In every way, there was no room to talk in detail, so all my diary entry says is, '*Went to Stanborough for the day. Went to the disco with Deb in the evening. Got off with Gary !!!!!??**!!! Deborah got off with Bill. Snigger. Bed at about 12.30. Tut Tut.*'

It was my Summer of Disco, and it began in May when I started going to the Brookmans Park Hotel, where a disco took place every Saturday and Monday night. I would often go twice a week, with a friend or with my cousin Marion. Punk was happening, but not yet for me, and not here, so instead we danced to soul records – 'For Once In My Life' by Stevie Wonder, 'Get Up Offa That Thing' by James Brown, 'Get Dancin'' by Disco Tex and the Sex-O-Lettes, although the whole point of the night was the moment when the DJ slowed things down and the dance floor would empty, girls to one side, boys to another, and we'd wait, staring at the floor or resolutely over the shoulder of any boy who might seem to be approaching, until one would mutter, 'Wanna dance?', without ever making eye contact, and we'd head back out for a slow dance. Hands on his shoulders to keep him at arms length if I wasn't sure, or clasped behind his neck if I was keener. And his hands would be on the back of my waist, or resting on my hips, or they'd slide down, and later I'd write 'WHT' in my diary, for 'Wandering Hand Trouble'.

31 May – *'Went to disco. Danced with this bloke who was about 6 foot 5.'*

The slow songs were always the same. 'If You Leave Me Now' by Chicago, 'I'm Not In Love' by 10cc, 'Without You' by Nilsson, and my favourite, 'Misty Blue' by Dorothy Moore. And I was only thirteen, but the boys were older, always older.

24 July – *'Creep asked me to dance again but I said no – found out he is called Tim and is a policeman! Yikes!!'*

I was thirteen, and he was a policeman. I keep thinking about what this means, and what it says about the time and the place. I picture myself, and I look like one of those girls in the *Top of the Pops* audiences, grinning at the camera, caught in the too-close embrace of an over-familiar DJ. I had shoulder-length hair, parted in the centre and with a fringe pushed back in wings that flicked out to either side of my forehead. The next layer of hair fell to the side of my head like spaniel's ears. I wore an A-line, knee-length denim skirt, with side pockets, and a wide, three-buttoned waistband, circled by a thin plastic belt. A peach-coloured T-shirt with a white collar, and on the front a print of a 1920s-style bob-haired beauty, like Daisy from *The Great Gatsby*. On my feet, a pair of denim sandals, rope soled, each foot bearing an appliqué butterfly. I was slim, but self-conscious; I was trying hard, but felt plain. Did I look thirteen, or even fourteen? I suspect that, to the men and boys I met, I just looked like a bird. Fair game. All the same.

31 July – *'Danced with boy I really fancied – blond hair, collarless shirt, really nice looking.'*

Sometimes the boys would say, 'D'you want to go outside?', which was code for a snog. I was slow-dancing with Gary when he said this. We went outside to the car park, where the air was immediately colder, and there was a patch of green between the hotel and the road to the station. He was dressed in a wide-collared shirt and tie, looking like one of the lads in *Gregory's Girl*. And we snogged and snogged while I kept my elbows pinned to my side, trying to stop him getting anywhere near my bra.

18 September – *'Went to disco. It was really good. Got off with Gary again. Got home about 11.15.'*

19 September – *'Saw Gary in his car, it's a dark green Cortina with 2 yellow stripes down the side.'*

I put the registration number in my diary too. I was nothing if not a stickler for detail. But the detail that screams at me now, though it apparently was not worthy of comment at the time, is the fact that he must have been at least seventeen. I've always complained bitterly about how strict my parents were, and yet that summer they didn't seem to have any idea what I was up to. Did the boys at the disco notice how young I was, or was everyone playing with fire, all the time? In every other aspect of my life, I was a child. Aside from the disco, my hobbies were walking the dog, playing badminton and piano lessons. I had a paper round. In September my periods started, and I circled the day in black in my diary.

25 September – *'Went to the disco. Saw Gary but he didn't ask me to dance. SOB.'*

The next day I turned fourteen. I think of myself wandering off out into the dark with this older boy who I didn't know at all, with his tie and his car, trying to look like a man. It seems weird, and somehow worse than thirteen-year-olds getting off with other thirteen-year-olds behind the bike sheds. More curious than confident, I had boundaries but no idea how to police them. I didn't know I was still a child, and the boys didn't care either way.

23 October – '*Went to the disco with Marion. Got off with Rod. Marion got off with his mate Martin. They both asked us out but we said no!!*'

30 October – '*Went to the disco with Marion. Danced with this mad bloke who thought I was a secretary.*'

The atmosphere of the disco – all mirrorball and Long Cool Screws and 'Get On Up' – conferred upon us all a kind of faux adulthood. The bar served us drinks, the boys asked us out.

6 November – '*Went to disco with Marion. Danced with two blokes – one grotty, second one, not bad at all!!!*'

13 November – '*Went to the disco with Liz. I danced with John. Talk about WHT!*'

In my diary it was all a joke. Nothing was real. September the 7th was my first day back at school, a new school year, and my periods started that morning, though I didn't say so. There's just the BLACK circle, when the rest of the diary is written in blue. I must have had to go and find a black pen. But all I wrote, in blue, was this: '*Back to school. Mrs Myers is our new form teacher. She's really nice – but*

37

MAD!! Had double science. Saw Spring and Autumn. Bed at about 9.'

Bed, wearing the uncomfortable belt and sanitary towel arrangement that Mum had given me. She didn't talk to me about periods, having described them to my sister Debbie a couple of years earlier, and presumably feeling that it was Debbie's responsibility, being two years older than me, to pass the information on. It would be a while before I found out about convenient stick-on Kotex pads, and even longer before I dared to go anywhere near a tampon. The first time I tried, with no help or instruction, it got stuck, and I spent an excruciating hour in the bathroom trying to remove it, fearing that I had removed essential parts of my insides along with it.

Mum never explained sex to me either. One day when I was off school sick, she gave me a book to read, full of information about puberty and chromosomes and intercourse. Words no one ever used. She left it with me for the day, and I glanced at it, curious, puzzled, embarrassed, and later she simply said, 'What did you make of it all? Pretty complicated isn't it, hahaha.' So we lived in an atmosphere where sex was invisible and ever-present, girls were both ignorant and fair game, there were rules and no rules, and everything was a joke. The day after my periods started, '*I watched Carry On Up the Khyber.*'

I think of the 1970s, and I think of children playing grown-up games. '*Me and Deb got followed home by 2 cheeky fellas! Saw George and Mildred. Bed at 10.*' The emotions in my diary are stylised, infantile, and yet I was on the cusp of something I knew nothing about.

11 September – *'In a mood cos Liz wasn't allowed to disco and we said we'd see GT there. I'm really FURIOUS and also BLUE. Bed at about 10.30. Sob sob . . .'*

There's a drawing of an eye, with teardrops falling from it. Which could be used in all sorts of circumstances. A week or so later, on the 20th of September: *'Had double cookery – made plum jam. Feeling fed up. 6 days till my birthday.'* Again, the crying eye. I think I liked drawing it. And on the 25th: *'Went to the disco – saw Gary but he didn't ask me to dance SOB.* [crying eye] *Feeling BLUE. Bed at about 11.30.'*

Next day was my fourteenth birthday. *'Got 2 LPs and 2 singles – Beach Boys, Eagles, Can, Jefferson Starship.'* And the year ended just as it began, with nothing happening. Or should I say, the next year started just the same. For here we are, heading into 1977, January the 1st, and what did I write in my diary? *'Went to Welwyn again but couldn't get any boots.'*

On a day towards the end of summer, in September 2017, I went on a walk with my sister Debbie, around the outskirts of Brookmans Park, to try to find out whether or not the Green Belt felt like countryside. I had realised that the fields and lanes and woods around the village were largely a mystery to me; that I had played on the fringes of them as a child but never walked there as an adult, and had no sense of whether it was at all rural, or whether it was merely an approximation of nature, a scaled-down, tamed version, something a very long way from those wild places beloved of nature writers.

In his book *Scarp*, the writer Nick Papadimitriou describes the area thus: 'A vast yet seemingly invisible presence hovers over the northern suburbs of London. Screened from the consciousness of the city dweller by the pressure of the day-to-day . . . the North Middlesex/ South Hertfordshire escarpment – or Scarp as I prefer to call it – broods and waits.' He goes on to say that 'Despite being some seventeen miles from east to west and attaining in excess of 400 feet above sea level in places, Scarp is seldom commented upon by either topographers or psychogeographers, and seemingly possesses no cultural currency.'

On the map at the front of his book are shaded areas that show where the land elevation is over 400 feet. There's a ridge to the west of Brookmans Park, reaching up towards North Mymms, and then another to the north-east of the village, stretching from the point on the Great North Road where the transmitting station is located, all the way to Newgate Street. It was a starting point at least, giving me a little germ of an idea: to see whether I could find any wild terrain, any landscape that felt other than suburban.

Debbie had come up to stay the night before, bringing her teenage diaries with her, and we'd sat up talking about them, and about her own memories of our family and of the village. Not as punctilious a diary-keeper as me, she had only three from her teens, and they all petered out halfway through the year. But still, they recorded a young version of me – aged eleven and pre-dating my own diaries – happily playing tennis every day, oblivious as yet to the sense that there was anything stifling about my surroundings. In her later teens though, many of her entries described dramas similar to those that appeared in mine: the same mood swings, the same rumbling discontent, the same need to break out.

She flicked through the one from 1980. 'Oh God, here's the final row, the one where I called Mum and Dad Nazis,' she said. She read the page out to me. It was pretty explosive, ending with the words, 'I will never ever forgive them for this, as long as I live.' And we rolled our eyes and laughed, remembering what had happened to inspire this fury, and what had happened afterwards.

She did forgive them, of course, and after she was married, they became close neighbours, spending every Christmas and several holidays together, Mum and Dad playing a huge role in the lives of her growing sons. In later years, she ended up living in the same building, in a flat on the floor above them, looking after both of them in their old age. A lot of forgiving and forgetting went on, as in so many families. We didn't want to be furious forever, and nor did they, so we moved on, all of us willing to sacrifice that boiling rage, and that desire to be right, for the greater good of family unity.

The day of the walk dawned, misty and drizzly, and we took the train up to Brookmans Park. Debbie hadn't been back for years. I had a map printed out, which traced a five-mile route around the village, taking in fields and woods and views. We assumed it would take us an hour and a half, and planned to be back in the village for lunch. Starting from the station, it led us down a lane, the route then doubling back on itself to take us onto a footpath running parallel to the railway track.

It was a good start to the walk. Trees arched over the path from either side, forming a long green tunnel that stretched away in front of us, almost resembling a holloway, that most rural of lanes, and making me think of Robert Macfarlane's book, *The Old Ways*, in which he describes walking ancient paths and undiscovered tracks. 'Maybe we're going to discover a kind of wilderness,' I thought, before noticing that already we had stumbled upon the remnants of what was clearly a popular meeting point for local teenagers. Litter clogged the hedgerow and under a tree lay scattered Coke cans, crisp packets, sandwich wrappers and a small, empty vodka bottle.

I sighed, and we carried on, coming out onto an open path, the damp grass soaking our trainers, blackberries ripening on the brambles at the side. A bridge crossed a small, dried-up brook, a continuation of Ray Brook which flows down from Gobions Wood, and off to our right was the veterinary college; a few sheep, and a couple of alpacas with early '80s haircuts, all shaved sides and floppy fringes, stared at us and stamped their front feet until we moved on.

Crossing a bridge over the railway, we walked back towards Brookmans Park, down the side of a ploughed field the colour of pencil lead. The soil was speckled with white, and covered in gulls. I remembered that I had always said there was no farming, but here I was being contradicted straight away. Debbie said she thought there was a farm nearby, up on Hawkshead Road. So I suppose I have to adjust my view and say, there was SOME farming.

Through the outskirts of the village again and then on to a narrow, nettley path which gave the impression of being rarely taken, and very much the road less travelled. Progress was slow and despite treading down as many nettles as we could, we got stung and scratched, and were grateful to reach the point where it opened out into Gobions Wood.

The walking here was beautiful – soft and dry underfoot, a woodland carpet of twigs, leaves and acorns, giving a slight crackle with every step. We came across a small, engraved metal plaque attached to a post, informing us that trees had been planted here in 1991 by children from our old primary school. Further on, two more plaques were dedicated to the memory of people who had loved these woods, and, looking closer, we realised we recognised the name of one of the families. 'In one of those diaries I was looking at last night,' said Debbie, 'I was planning to go to a party given by their son, but then something happened, and I never got there.' It all felt very familiar, as if nothing had changed since we lived there, thirty-something years ago, and as if all the same neighbours were still present.

Lulled into a sense of security, we then made our fatal mistake and took a wrong turn. Misreading our directions, and mistrusting our instincts, we went one way and then turned back, feeling that our initial choice had been wrong. Heading off into another section of the wood, which suddenly seemed to be much bigger than we remembered, we both realised we'd never been in this part before, never even knew it was here. Twenty years we'd lived in the village, and here we were, in completely new territory. And we were hopelessly lost.

Tracing circles, we would follow a path only to have it fork in two, choosing one direction, then returning to choose the other. Reaching the edge of the trees, we would find no way out, just a field bordered with barbed wire, and so we'd head back in. We passed a dried-up riverbed, which had been dammed up with thick black tree trunks; a mysterious brick tunnel leading who knows where; plank bridges over rivulets and streams. The day had warmed up and the air was heavy and humid, the ground lightly steaming. The woodland felt ancient, primeval, the opposite of suburban. And we were getting hungry.

Finally, after maybe an hour of fruitless wandering, we spotted a red jacket in the distance and sped towards it, calling out 'Hallo? Excuse me?' feeling very like Withnail coming across the farmer, and in panicky voice asking: 'Are you the farmer? We've gone on holiday by mistake.' Being set on the right track, we yet managed to go wrong one more time, until finally the path led us back to the spot where we'd made our first mistake, over an hour ago.

It was the weirdest feeling, to have been so lost in a place so close to our old home and yet so unknown to us. Within ten minutes of finding our way out of the wood, we were on the Great North Road – once the main road to the north of England, and a known turnpike or toll road for several hundred years – with the familiar tower of the transmitting station looming above us. And five minutes after that we were in the Cock of the North pub, where Mum and Dad used to go for their annual wedding anniversary dinner and at no other time during the year.

We were chastened. Honestly, if we couldn't even find our way around here, what chance would we have navigating the Pennine Way or crossing Dartmoor? What did it say about us and our skills, that we were so hopeless in even this suburban version of the natural world? Because, in truth, the walk never had felt like real countryside. There were almost always houses in view, or roads within earshot. Trains hurtling past somewhere in the distance. The woods had defeated us, and momentarily seemed wild, but that was more down to our stupidity and map-reading failure than anything else.

We walked back down into the village, and went for a final restorative cup of tea in the hotel. Sitting in the bar area, we looked around and realised it was a new conversion of the old function room, the very space where the disco used to be held. As we sat there with our tea, Marvin Gaye's 'Got To Give It Up' came on in the background. 'I used to go out to parties / And stand around / Cause I was too nervous / To really get down'.

And suddenly we were fifteen and seventeen again, up in our bedrooms listening to Greg Edwards on Capital Radio, getting ready to go out to a party or a disco on a Saturday night. 'But my body yearned to be free / I got up on the floor and thought / Somebody could choose me.' We'd have been fired up, excited, dancing and running back-and-forth between our two bedrooms. Swapping lip gloss. 'Can I borrow your white loafers?' Sharing our Anais Anais perfume. Trying on a belt. Calling out, 'Where's my nail polish remover?' Spraying our hair, and, oh dear no, not country girls at all. Not at all.

By 1943 the population of Brookmans Park was 2,300, and developers still had aspirations for a population of 7,500 when urban planners finally began to commit to the idea of the Green Belt. It had been a long time coming, and the notion of preserving a ring of open greenery around London, preventing urban sprawl by restricting building and development, had been around since about 1890. A 'Development Plan for Greater London' was proposed by the London Society in 1919, arguing for a two-mile-wide buffer zone. It wasn't until the Town and Country Planning Act of 1947 that the plans for a Green Belt became formalised, in an attempt to stop London expanding outwards, securing a band of countryside around it.

But how did this affect somewhere like Brookmans Park? As a suburb, it wasn't sprawling out from the city, instead it had sprung up in an apparently empty green space, within easy reach of London. Its qualities were to do with the combination of these two factors – rural beauty along with accessibility to urban jobs. The idea of the Green Belt would protect the rural space between it and the city, but also acted as a brake on the development of the place itself, which still was only half built.

The 1943 Greater London Plan (which included Hertfordshire) looked at Brookmans Park and drew the following damning conclusions – 'The development here consists of an entirely unfinished dormitory estate based upon the railway station, with a small shopping centre at the station . . . That any growth whatsoever should have occurred here is to be most strongly deplored . . . The houses that have been erected should have been built at Potters Bar itself where they could have been welded and blended into the existing town life. Further expansion at Brookmans Park should be most rigidly controlled.'

In other words, Brookmans Park should never have happened at all. The district council objected and development continued, another 200 houses getting approval in 1946, but the end was in sight, and government opposition was building. In 1946 approval for some development was revoked because it infringed on the Green Belt, and a small factory proposal met with objections and was prevented. In 1950 the primary school was built, opening in autumn 1951 with 110 children, and in 1959 another 100 houses were approved, but other plans were rejected.

What this meant was that the growth of Brookmans Park suddenly stopped, preserving it in aspic – a place with no history and no future. There was nothing very old (the earliest houses were from 1927) and nothing very new (building stopped completely in 1959). To this day, there is still debate in and around Brookmans Park about new housing proposals. There is a desire to stop Brookmans

Park itself expanding, and filling in the green space between it and London, but the Green Belt also aims to stop towns and villages merging into each other. In effect, a place like Brookmans Park has a little Green Belt around itself. It's a castle, surrounded by a moat, shutting out the rest of the world, the barbarian hordes.

I've always loved London. It seemed far, far away, and yet now I realise that Brookmans Park was locked into a symbiotic relationship with it. The village only existed because of the city, was built solely for commuters, and so they were inextricably linked. I lived on what was effectively one of Planet London's moons, and each exerted a gravitational pull on the other, although for me, the force emanating from the city was much stronger, magnetically drawing me towards it.

I remember a school trip, when I was perhaps eleven or twelve, and we came on a coach up to the British Museum. It was a sunny day, towards the end of the summer term, and though I don't recall the museum at all, I do remember driving into the city, and the streets getting busier, and the green of Regents Park, and then parking somewhere and walking along the pavement, sun filtering through the plane trees, the air dusty and hot, fragrant with exhaust fumes, and loving everything about being there, the feel of the place, the smell of it, and thinking 'I WILL LIVE HERE.'

In the mid nineteenth century, my rural ancestors, Job and

Miriam Bush, upped sticks and moved, with several of their children, from a Norfolk village to St Pancras in London. There they carried on in the market garden business, working at Covent Garden, and driving produce around the city. By 1891 their son Frederick and his family were living in Litcham Street in Kentish Town, which, by the end of the century had become one of the worst of the slum streets in the area; much of it was demolished in the 1920s. Another of their sons, James, married and settled in the Old Kent Road, before moving to Kentish Town, where he had a son, also named James, who was my great-grandfather. In 1899, this particular James married Edith Bell, at St Pancras Parish Church on Euston Road, as I never fail to point out to whoever I am with whenever I pass it. He was my mum's grandfather, and she remembered him as a good sportsman, a runner and a boxer, who used to drive pairs of horses from Whitestone Pond in Hampstead into central London for a bet.

On Dad's side, my great-great-grandfather William Julius Thorn was in Chelsea in the 1870s, working as a commercial clerk, and later as a domestic gardener. They too moved to north London, and later my dad's mother would be born in another street in Kentish Town, St Leonards Square, only yards away from the streets – Marsden Street, Rhyl Street, Weedington Road – where all my mother's family lived. In a very small area of London, I can point out to you – on every corner – churches where ancestors of mine were wed, streets where they were born. And yet my parents left, meaning that my childhood happened elsewhere, and although I moved back as soon as I could, in the 1980s, it makes me feel that London is both in my blood and not. I am of the place, and not of it, and I feel or imagine sentimental connections at every twist and turn. I have a great-great-grandfather who was baptised at St Pancras Old Church, which is now used for live music, and where I have sat in the audience and watched Ben perform a gig, imagining all the time that I could feel some ancient connection with the very walls, the air we were breathing, the stones beneath.

A few years ago I went on a walking tour of Aldgate, the tour guide being someone I was in a band with aged seventeen. He loves London as much as I do, which confirms my belief that growing up just outside predisposes you to overlook its faults and dwell forever on its beauty and allure. So if you love the place, you will find beauty in, for instance, the contemplation of the spot where a plague pit was dug behind the church of St Botolph without Aldgate. The small group of us on the tour stood there on a Saturday afternoon, as the traffic roared by, lost in the past, surrounded by ghosts, suffused with the feeling that everyone who has ever lived in this city is somehow still here. That feeling continued, grew stronger even, as we moved on to Wilton's Music Hall, dating from the 1850s (did any of my ancestors go there, I wondered?) and to Cable Street, where we swelled with undeserved pride, basking in the memory of the locals who stopped fascists in their tracks. Then in Altab Ali Park, named after a young Bangladeshi clothing worker who was murdered in 1978 on his way home from work, our spirits fell a little, and we realised that maybe the fascists weren't stopped after all. Maybe they never are, not completely.

Outside the Whitechapel Gallery, which for the last hundred years has housed exhibitions from Picasso to Pollock, our guide quoted John Ruskin at us – 'Life without industry is guilt, and industry without art is brutality' – and on that stirring note, with all the stories of the afternoon ringing in our ears, we retired to the Halal Restaurant, which was established in 1939 and so is the oldest Indian eatery in east London, and finally to the Oliver Conquest, a pub which was once the bar of the original Garrick Theatre, and which now offers more than 160 varieties of gin. We sampled too many of them of course, and paid the price next day. The bathtub gin did me in, and the night ended in slightly more Hogarthian style than we might have intended, but really, what could be more London? God love and preserve the place. When I got home, I wrote a song called 'Smoke', in which I tried to sum up all the complicated feelings I have about this city, few of them wholly rational, all of them suffused with a sense of longing and belonging.

> London you're in my blood
> And you've been there for so long
> London you're in my blood
> But I feel you going wrong.

1977

A blue Collins diary, with four days to two pages, allowing five or six sentences per day. I was fourteen, and nothing much had changed yet. I ate 1970s food, *'Got up about 10.30 and had a lovely fried breakfast. Had roast beef for dinner. Got a Creme egg in the afternoon yummee'*, and then I went on a 1970s health kick . . .

6 February 1977 – *'Liz and I have decided to go healthy – doing exercises, going for walks, drinking PLJ. Went to bed early at 9.30.'* Next day Liz was ill and off school, but I carried on regardless . . .

8 February – *'Took dog for a walk and did loads more exercises.'*

13 February – *'I went for THREE walks.'* It fizzled out after a while, as I got distracted by other interests. By May the actual exercise – *'Rode down to Liz's at 7.30, and we went jogging in the fields at the end of her road. It was really lovely down there.'* – gave way to this kind of thing: *'Went jogging with Liz again. On the way down there 2 gorgeous blokes followed me in their car and said hello, whistled etc'*, *'on the way to school the 2 blokes with*

the blue Saab who live above Taylors were waving and shouting to me'.

The days were still filled with school and telly. I watched *The Goodies, Porridge, Are You Being Served?* and *The Six Million Dollar Man . . . Doctor on the Go, TOTP, Tom O'Connor* and *Mike Yarwood . . . The Muppet Show, Happy Days, Roots, Jesus of Nazareth* and *Rising Damp . . . The Streets of San Francisco, Planet of the Apes, The Rockford Files, Rhoda* and *Van Der Valk*. All of us still watching together and watching the same programmes as our neighbours. Far off in the future, unimaginable to us then, lay the world we now live in, where parents and children view separately and privately, so that, for instance on the night my husband Ben and I sat down to watch the first episode of a new series of *House of Cards*, which opened in a prison cell, with a character we'd met before on a top bunk talking to himself, no, wait, reciting some kind of porn scenario, and the camera panned down to the bunk below, where his cell mate was furiously masturbating, and I do mean FURIOUSLY, so that Ben and I both glanced anxiously at the sitting-room door, hoping no kids were about to walk through it, on a night like this I couldn't help thinking, 'Thank God we hardly ever watch telly as a family any more.' And we counted our blessings that current parents and teens have been spared the gritted-teeth communal viewing of TV sex scenes, all staring resolutely ahead, wishing for the ground to open up.

It was a formative and scarring experience for anyone my age, even though the scenes involved were tamer than the one described above. If I say '*Bouquet of Barbed Wire*', most people in their fifties will know exactly what I mean, and I'm sure everyone has their own personal example. I remember one Christmas my granddad striding over to the telly to turn it off with the vigour of a man twenty years younger, because of snogging in the film *Love Story*. Not actual sex, just snogging. Separate tellies, laptops and the internet have saved us from this. 'Times have changed, Lord Grantham,' one of my kids said to Ben recently, when he was complaining about something, and of course we're not the prudes our grandparents, or even parents, were. I can talk to my kids about sex (if I have to), but I'm still glad I didn't have to watch that opening *House of Cards* scene with them next to me on the sofa.

Back in 1977 I bought records by Archie Bell and the Drells, the Three Degrees, and Deniece Williams; I '*got some sheet music from Delmars,* Say a Little Prayer*, and* Yellow Brick Road'; I read *Love Story*, *Carrie*, *The Day of the Locust*, *The Sting* and *The Great Gatsby* ('*it's great*'). Also *Jackie* magazine, *Pink* and *Oh Boy*, and I started working a Saturday job in the post office, earning £1.75 on my first morning.

I'd stopped going to the disco, and so experienced something of a boy drought at the beginning of the year, but then the house parties started, where instead of complete strangers, and policemen with their own cars, I got off with boys I knew, who were more my own age. First one boy from the posher end of Brookmans Park, then a boy from up the road. In May there was a disco in Welham Green: '*It wasn't bad I suppose, if you LIKE half empty discos with no booze.'* And in June, a party in Cuffley: *'it was more like a mass brawl/orgy. Party got a bit (??) out of control.'* In August, we went on holiday to Wales, taking my friend Liz along, and at a disco I got off with a boy called Jay, meeting up with him the following night. *'Jay's really called Jean Paul, he's half French, and in the army. Got off with him again. Walked me home.'* I was still only fourteen, and he was in the army, what was it about men in uniform with me? The next evening he got off with someone else at the disco, and I was upset. When we returned home from the holiday, I wrote, *'Seems strange that I'll never see Jay again, and I miss him a bit. Still it was horrible of him to arrange to meet me and then turn up with another girl!! Oh well it was nice while it lasted, now I'd better just forget him . . .'* The arc of a love affair, concertinaed into four days.

And suddenly, out of nowhere, glimpses of punk, like little flickers of light, pulsing on and off in the gloom, barely noticed at first, not bright enough to fully catch my eye. At a disco in St Albans in June, *'Not bad records, Supertramp, Stranglers, Sex Pistols, Jacksons, Alessi'*, and in July, *'Liz came over in the afternoon and we wandered about a bit . . . Mum and Dad went to a tennis club dance in Welham Green. Listened to an interview with Johnny Rotten.'* By the end of the month I was buying singles by Dr Feelgood and The Jam, and coincidentally, or perhaps not, I began to notice for the first time that my life was dull and limited.

27 August – *'This diary's getting very boring, something better happen soon.'*

28 August – *'Nothing really happened today. Well, nothing concerning blokes. Wish someone would have a party, I feel like going out. I'm getting fed up with sitting around all the time!! Where's all the night life gone?'*

I'd go to any party or disco that popped up, but never seemed to meet anyone new. We would all get off with each other in rotation, but none of it ever led anywhere. Stuck, and with limited options, I got fixated on one boy after another, banking everything on them being the one to change things, make something happen.

2 September – *'If I don't get off with him soon I'll go MAD, LOONY, ROUND THE BEND . . . Shouldn't think I ever will though, so loony bin, here I come . . . '*

This couldn't last; it was hopelessly passive of me. I started a Saturday job in the supermarket, *'priced things, packed shelves, they even let me work the till. Got £3.60.'* And with that money I started buying lots and lots of records. The boredom was beginning to act as a catalyst; new friends were emerging, new interests, and I was leaving behind the crowd of people from Brookmans Park. By the end of 1977 I had turned fifteen, built up a head full of frustration and a head full of steam, and amid the boredom I was beginning to be excited. There are lots of diary entries about records I've bought, and who I've seen on the telly.

And luckily I wasn't too cool or too much of a punk to enjoy something as conventional as Christmas Day. *'Yahoo, Xmas Day. Got LOADS of really great presents – £25, Rats LP, Jam LP, Boots token, record token, diary, ring, earrings, necklace, toilet bag set, legwarmers. Ate and drank all day. Saw* Funny Girl. *Had a really lovely day. Went to bed about 1 o'clock.'*

There are moments in my teenage diaries where I barely recognise the person who wrote them, and other times when she seems completely and utterly the person I am now. At this particular moment, I feel I could look in the mirror and see myself reflected, younger but still the same, and I could say to this 1977 version of myself: 'Tracey, you're fifteen now, and you're growing up and you're changing, but you're never going to change that much. You're never going to stop loving Christmas Day. You will one day write a song with a sarky Christmas reference, "Come on Home", in which you'll sing, "Every day's like Christmas Day without you / It's cold and there's nothing to do" – which will lead to near-ostracism from your Christmas-loving family. "Oh no, Tracey hasn't got her tree up yet, she HATES Christmas," they'll say, arms folded and looking at you, as you weakly protest, for several years, that it was meant as a joke. But then when your kids come along something inside you will click back to an automatic pre-programmed setting, and you'll set about recreating in intricate detail the Christmases of childhood, which went like clockwork, set in motion by Mum, and ran to a schedule as precise as a Swiss railway timetable. Reliable, repetitive, reassuring – everything that children love life to be – they consisted of the same events happening in exactly the same order every year, so that you could set your watch by the delivery of special drinks (Advocaat, Tizer), the appearance of a box of Eat Me dates, the arrival of Grandad in a three-piece suit, penknife poised and ready to take the peel off an apple in one single strip. And you'd eat a Chocolate Orange on Christmas afternoon, and Matchmakers in the evening, and NEVER THE OTHER WAY ROUND. That's how it was. You won't forget.'

Brookmans Park was designed to be self-sufficient, but so successful was this that it created a feeling of isolation, even though it was not far from anywhere, turning it into an island floating in a sea of fields. I live in north London now, and Brookmans Park seems miles and miles away. It is fifty minutes on the train. Yet the sense of distance is overwhelming, lost in space and time, psychologically distant. In truth, it feels faintly fictional to me. There is a gulf between now and the past, just as there is a gulf between town and country. Between me now, and me then.

During the brief period when I was a driver, about twenty-five years ago, I drove to Brookmans Park a few times, but despite having often made the journey as a passenger, I always got hopelessly lost. Each time I drove right past it and had to turn back to take the correct exit off the A road. A Freudian might read something into this.

As a child, I had no sense at all that London was nearby. But the village didn't just feel far from London, it also felt far from other places that were actually close by. Knebworth was only two stops past Welwyn Garden City on the train, and yet going there for the festival, I remember it now as a trip into the deep wilds of the countryside, like Glastonbury or Woodstock. Perhaps the reason that we felt cut off even from nearby villages was that Brookmans Park itself had everything you could need, in a way that was both wonderful and awful. Clustered around the village green were the shops, walkable from our house. There was a petrol station and garage for repairs. A GP and a dentist, a church, a primary school AND a secondary school, the Brookmans Park Hotel, with its bar and off-licence, and six rooms for guests.

All this for a population of just over 3,000 people. There wasn't much choice, but there was one of EVERYTHING you needed. And there is the downside. Being so self-contained makes a place insular and claustrophobic. The village gave the impression of not needing anyone else, or anything else; incurious about the world, it gradually became dismissive, and disapproving of the world. There is a sneery description of suburbia that defines it as a place devoid of higher education and devoid of culture. Brookmans Park could defend itself against the first charge by stating that it at least had a respected veterinary college, but the second accusation is impossible to refute: there was no cinema, no theatre, no music venue and – perhaps worse than that – no sense that such things were important.

So what were we to do? For teenagers, there was the village green, where local tough kids sat smoking. It was a vaguely transgressive spot, despite being in the centre of the village, in full view of everyone. I longed to go and smoke there, hanging around with the kind of kids who gave off an intangible air of delinquency, shouting and shoving each other, but it was absolutely forbidden. The only other diversions on offer were the non-arty, supposedly healthy pursuits of tennis and golf. There was a tennis club at the end of a wooded lane at the top end of the village, a dusty clubhouse where you could help yourself to an orange squash, and an annual tournament where the singles cup would be contested by the local alpha girls with ponytails and pristine whites.

And there was the golf club, where the village's insularity was expressed in a nastier way. The feeling of being separate and not having to keep pace with the times meant that you could defy progress and end up on the wrong side of historical arguments. This was the situation at the golf club, membership of which was aspirational. Acceptance meant not just the freedom to play a round of golf, but admission into a social group, and in order for it to be exclusive it had to exclude. I remember being told that our beloved village GP, who was Jewish, could not join and had to drive to Potters Bar to play. The club there had been founded in 1923 by a successful fur merchant, William Ponikwer, who loved golf but, being Jewish too, could not find a club he was allowed to join within easy reach of London. But that was the 1920s. How could such a situation still be tolerated forty or fifty years later? It was glossed over, but struck me – a teenager who was learning about racism, and by 1978 marching against the National Front – as monstrous, unforgivable.

I was forever running into those kinds of brick walls, making too much of a fuss about things that no one else seemed bothered by. I took things too seriously, in a way that didn't fit. In my house, we weren't a religious family, but as children we all attended Sunday School, and we'd sometimes go to midnight mass on Christmas Eve. Then, as a teenager, it was suggested that I join the social group called the Table Fellowship, which involved Sunday church-going.

I was resistant. A 1978 diary entry reads, '*Mum keeps going on at me to join the Table Fellowship, but I don't want to and it's beginning to get on my nerves now.*' I suspect this was more because I thought church was uncool than anything else, but I certainly dug my heels in. The vicar came round to our house to talk to me, but I hid upstairs. Meanwhile, down in the lounge he patiently explained to my mum that you didn't have to be religious; you could just play table tennis. But I took the moral high ground, claiming to find it hypocritical in the way that only teenagers can find things hypocritical.

It held no allure for me, offered no spiritual significance, and I was yearning for significance, looking everywhere for it. The laid-back approach of the vicar was almost designed to put me off. I wanted passion and commitment. If he'd said, 'You have to believe all of this with every fibre of your being, and sign HERE and HERE, in BLOOD', I might have been more interested, but instead he offered youth club evenings, modern hymns accompanied by tambourines, a pantomime at Christmas. The nondescript post-war building was not designed to attract the poetically minded, having no ancient stones, no tower, no ancestral family pews, no brass plates commemorating the gallant dead of the First World War. Perhaps most significantly, there was, and still is, no churchyard. No one is buried there. No gravestones to gather moss or summon the grieving. The burials happened at North Mymms instead, in the 700-year-old churchyard. Out of sight, out of mind.

I think of Philip Larkin's poem 'Churchgoing', in which he ponders the meaning and importance of churches to an increasingly secular society. In the end he concludes that churches will never become completely obsolete,

> Since someone will forever be surprising
> A hunger in himself to be more serious,
> And gravitating with it to this ground,
> Which, he once heard, was proper to grow wise in,
> If only that so many dead lie round.

But what if no dead lie round? What if they've all been taken somewhere else, and you're being told you don't have to believe in anything very much to join the church group, and no one seems to be interested in the arts, and everyone votes Tory and the golf club is racist, what then?

In 1986, the villagers of Brookmans Park took part in something called the 'Domesday Project'. Published by the BBC, to mark 900 years since William the Conqueror's Domesday Book, it was an attempt to document everyday life, to collect stories about 'the ordinary rather than the extraordinary' and preserve them for future generations. In order to come up with this record, the UK was divided up into 23,000 separate areas, each measuring 4×3 kilometres, called Domesday Squares, or 'D-Blocks'. One of those D-Blocks was Brookmans Park, and it was the children of the primary school who went to work, gathering information via questionnaires, and submitting their written reports, which are a charming mixture of fact and impression, objective truth and somewhat naive opinion.

For me, it's a fascinating snapshot of what life was like in the village just a few years after I'd left, proving that, still, almost nothing had changed: I could have written most of the descriptions myself apart from a few rare occasions of novelty which leap out at me.

The children begin by describing how they had gone about their task: 'We did not have as much time as we would have liked as we went to Paris on a school trip in June and a lot of this term was spent doing work on that.' (Paris on a school trip! In my day, we went to Swanage.) 'We did several questionnaires which we sent out to people in the village. We were surprised at how few people bothered to return them. It was just over half of those we sent out.' Of course, just over half sounds like a reasonable turnout to me, but seeing the children's obvious enthusiasm run aground on typical adult indifference is a bit heartbreaking.

Overall, they paint a picture of life in the 1980s being lived more or less as it had been in the 1960s. A village policeman still rode around on his bicycle; a familiar figure, known to all. 'He helps to run the Youth Centre and takes part in any pantomimes or musicals that are put on in the village,' presumably when he's taking a break from dealing with the rare, but quite unexpectedly exciting crimes: 'In June 1985 a petrol filling station on the A1000 was robbed and the attendant was driven away as a hostage. Two months earlier a newsagent was robbed by two youths who escaped in a car.'

The children describe the scheme whereby residents are asked to keep an eye on each other's houses as 'the local neighbourly watch campaign', and they also find out about the village politics which swirl around issues of planning permission and building: 'There is a Green Belt Society which watches demands for planning very carefully. It costs £1 a year to belong and at the meetings they decide what action needs taking to stop development. There was a meeting in July 1985 when it was learned that a property developer had applied for permission to build over a hundred houses on green land near the village. The local rate payers' association took up the fight and there are plans to collect money to buy the land for the village so that it would be impossible to build on it.'

I can picture that kind of meeting. Voices raised, the hissing of local outrage. On the one hand, there's something admirably collectivist about them banding together to buy the land, but on the other hand you can't help wondering what they might have then done with it. Perhaps put up a fence, or a wall, and lots of Keep Out signs? That devotion to the Green Belt ideal can be a bit Little Englander, a bit Nimby. To some it is a sacrilegious idea, but I can't help wondering whether those fields should be built on. Brookmans Park is so well placed, with good roads and transport links, and shops that were designed for a larger population – would a hundred houses on green land have ruined it? Wouldn't there still be plenty of woods and fields nearby, for those who needed a glimpse of a view, or a Sunday walk? Perhaps the opposition wasn't unconnected to the fact that increased housing stock might bring down the inflated local house prices.

Whatever the motivation, the villagers were planning to take matters into their own hands to protect themselves from the threat of incoming developers, perhaps because they had got used to feeling that the place belonged to them, and that it both was their right and duty to defend it against incomers bringing change. Even in 1986, 'many of the roads in the village are private and are repaired by the people who live there'. They were used to doing things themselves, and not liking the way outsiders did them.

Then the children visited a local farm. I know. I said there weren't any farms, didn't I? And then Debbie pointed one out to me on our walk. It strikes me that I'm talking about an imaginary place as much as a real one. If memory skews our perception, then the village I recall is semi-fictional, and I have to accept that my account isn't neutral, or wholly truthful; it's one-sided and irrational, constructed out of my experiences and my reaction, sometimes over-reaction, to them. And this farm they visited, which I had edited out of my memory, having no interest in it, consisted of 200 acres of oats, wheat and barley, 150 cows and a bull, four tractors, a combine harvester and a slurry tank. The children noted that 'Mr Morgan, the farmer, has been farming here for forty years and complains that even though he uses his land to the full he finds it difficult to make a reasonable profit. In this last year he made £4,000 less than the previous year.'

The villagers, with their insistence on ownership and privacy, and determination to keep up the high standards, didn't have much time for those who couldn't keep up. So what would happen to someone who was struggling? Here is the brutal reality: 'There is really nobody without work here as all the people in the village have very expensive houses and run expensive cars. We did a survey and found that most of the people work in London . . . If people do lose their jobs they do not stay here but move away.'

They move away. The candour of that last statement reveals that it could only have been written by a child. It paints a picture of a place which could only be a home, a safe haven, as long as you could afford it. Entirely uniform in its social make-up, with a high degree of homogeneity, it had no place for anyone who slipped. It's the great problem that had existed since the village was first built, with so little in the way of affordable housing, so little variety, so little inclusiveness.

This isn't healthy for a society, is it? It's not good for a place and its inhabitants to be so unvarying, to be so impervious to change. For what shines out from the children's portrait of the village is its apparent immutability. 'We interviewed several people who live in or near Brookmans Park and the interesting thing was that we were told the same by all of them. The village and its surroundings have not changed a lot since they have lived here.' Indeed.

One final section describes a typical day in the life of one of the children, and reads like a page from my diaries:

'On Monday morning it's hard to get me up and get ready for school. I wash, dress and have toast for breakfast. After putting my coat and shoes on, my mum drives me to school in her blue Mini Metro. It's not very far to walk but I never have enough time to walk. After the whistle goes in the playground we all line up for assembly. The whole school goes into the hall. We usually have a story and a hymn. Then we go back to our class for lessons. We have maths first and after morning break English. Sometimes we do Science or topic when we can write about anything we like. At lunchtime we have a school meal. Most people have it but some bring a packed lunch. After school is over I go home, have tea and watch television. My favourite programme is *The A Team*.'

It sounds perfect. And after all, children never really change. This is just a child's life being described. No surprise that it sounds mundane and conventional, routine and cosy. I was equally content as a child. I wonder what a teenager would have said. Would there have been the same howl of anguish as is soon to come in my teenage diaries? The same discontent? And would there still be today?

2016

I walk down to Peplins Way, to the house I was born in, (front bedroom, 1962), and grew up in – like all children taking my home for granted, thinking it permanent, and as old as the hills. Even though there weren't any hills. Not much change from when I left, though the house next door looks in need of care and attention. I carry on down the road and past the huge playing field of the primary school, hedged by hawthorn and dog rose. There's the concrete where we French skipped and chalked out hopscotch, and where I was bullied one day and bullied someone else on another. Where we chanted our way through clapping games. A sailor went to sea sea sea to see what he could see see see. I ell oh vee ee love you, I kay eye double ess kiss you, I ell oh vee ee, kay eye double ess, will you marry me? Still standing in the playground is the high wall where older boys used to sit and dangle their legs. I thought health and safety might have knocked it down, it was always an accident waiting to happen. I walk around the block to the front of the school, and count twenty-one cars in the car park. I don't remember there ever being any.

On the village green, four teenage girls are sitting on the bench in over-the-knee socks and school blazers. They might have been there for forty years. They seem like ghosts. They might be me and my sister. Me and my cousin. Older girls who sat there before us. But they're not ghosts, and the atmosphere in the village isn't ghostly, it's bustly – shoppers shopping, scaffolding going up on a house, tree surgeons pruning a willow. I look at the North Mymms Parish Council noticeboard, which has a Neighbourhood Watch poster, and a photo of the MP for Welwyn Hatfield, the Right Honourable Grant Shapps, with his email address in case you want to contact or troll him. There are dates and agendas of forthcoming parish council meetings, names of councillors – all the Brookmans Park members being Conservatives. (Later on I check the Brexit voting result, and in the referendum the borough voted Leave by 31,060 votes to Remain's 27,550. In contrast, the borough of Camden, where I live now, voted Remain by 71,295 votes, to Leave's 23,838.)

As I walk away from the green, I notice the lack of large, established trees. It seems deliberate, the planting of small species. Prunus, crab apples, small silver birches. The houses are all two storeys high, and few trees stand any higher than the rooftops, and everything, compared to London, is so low that it's as if there's a lid on it. Nothing anywhere seems to reach up to the sky, and there's a smallness, and a feeling of newness, even now, after 80 years. A lack of history, of anything grown in or embedded – of maturity? When I walk up the hill towards Gobions Wood, I see two big horse chestnuts and, at last, two proper

73

huge oaks, and the shade they cast, the overhang of leaves and branches, is comforting and protective. There's finally a sense of stature, an unapologetic grandeur, an acceptance of nature being bigger than us, towering over us.

1978

A Letts diary with a blue cover, still only pocket-sized, but a page a day now giving room for at least ten sentences per entry. I'm fifteen years old. Something had happened to my general outlook and attitude, perhaps a heady mix of punk and hormones, and it had infected my sensibility to the point where more or less everything was described as 'boring'. Although, despite this, I was still watching, and enjoying, the same old programmes on the telly, and I was a huge fan of *Coronation Street*.

9 January 1978 – '*Saw* Coronation Street, *tres exciting, Ernest Bishop got shot! WOW!!*'

11 January – '*Saw* Coronation Street, *Ernest Bishop died!! God, it was so exciting!!*'

Current events rarely intruded into my little world, as I was a typically solipsistic teenager, and even when they did, my reaction was only to note the personal effect on me and my boring life. This was a time of economic and industrial turmoil. I know now that the company my dad worked for was in trouble, and in order not to lose his job I think he took a pay cut, which affected our lifestyle, and my parents' ability to continue their aspirational rise. So for instance, we had few holidays and life was pretty spartan. But on the other hand, strikes and power cuts were great fun.

8 February – '*FANTASTIC NEWS – because of the oil strike there's no heating at school now so we haven't got to go in again until at least Tuesday, hooray.*'

24 February – '*The oil was delivered today BOO HISS so school's back to normal on Monday (damn).*'

12 February – '*Saw* The London Weekend Show. *It was all about kids who burn down their schools, hahaha. Had chicken for lunch. Deb went to choir. Had a biccy for supper. Went to bed about 10 and listened to Luxy for a while.*'

If it had been written yet, I could have walked around all day singing that Del Amitri song 'Nothing Ever Happens'. But I can see now that the boredom was inspirational as well as dispiriting, and that there was a generational element to my predicament, mine being one of the last for whom there was such a limited amount of entertainment on offer that we had to resort to the cliché of making our own, which of course may have been a good thing in the long run. Nothing amuses my children more than hearing me recite a list of all the things we had to do without. No recording of TV programmes you missed. No films on

DVD to watch when you chose. No internet, or computer, or phone, obviously, but also no TV channels beyond ITV, and no TV AT ALL after closedown each night. The very idea of closedown! Of being said good night to, reminded to turn your telly off, and then played the national anthem and sent to bed. It all sounds to them like one long punishment, as if for the whole of the '70s we were all essentially grounded (a word we never used).

Our access to clothes was equally limited, so when it came to looking punky, I couldn't just go up to Top Shop and buy the outfit. Urban clothes shops like Sex or Seditionaries were scary and expensive for a girl like me, so we had to make the outfits ourselves out of whatever we could get our hands on. When I went to see XTC at St Albans City Hall in February, '*I wore straight jeans, long shirt, jacket, tie, badges, sunglasses*' – which sounds as if I probably looked a bit like Captain Sensible. In March I '*bought Jennie Waters' blazer for £5*'. Later that month, '*Katrina lent me her Lou Reed album. We all tried to think up mad outfits to wear for tomorrow night. I'm wearing track suit trousers, Dad's shirt, plimsolls, tie, jacket.*'

It's easy to forget how DIY and makeshift our style was. My kids can go out and buy more or less anything that's in fashion, either new and cheap, or vintage and cheap. Everything is easy to source, and for a price you can have whatever you want, right away. Currently, on fashion website Net-a-Porter, you can buy a Sonic Youth T-shirt for £250.

We'd be thwarted by lack of transport too, and oh, the effort we made to get anywhere. We'd go up to London on the bus for the day, using Red Rover tickets, and a simple night out could turn into an adventure, an excursion, an act of creativity and determination involving timetables and cancellations, missed trains and buses, the endless searching for someone who could provide a lift. In March, I wrote all week long about a party on the Saturday night, what I was going to wear, who'd be there, only for Saturday to finally come around and *'Didn't go to the party cos we couldn't get there or back.'* In a moment of supreme bathos, *'Saw* The Professionals. *It was really good.'*

My diary is a bit cagey about it, but at this point, in desperation, I started going once a week or so to Rangers meetings, hanging out with a group of boys who were Venture Scouts. We played darts and table tennis, did yoga one week, and had a talk from a probation officer. I learned how to put up a tent, and change the wheel on a car, and later in the summer we went canoeing. I was writing about the Sex Pistols all the time, but also learning how to tie knots. On May the 1st, the day after attending the big Anti-Nazi League rally in Victoria Park, I went to a disco at the British Legion in Potters Bar.

It was also very unpunk of me, but I was forever sunbathing that summer, and commenting on how brown I was. I should have been aiming for a pasty pallor, but instead, I very much liked having a tan. This had somewhat naff connotations, maybe still does. I think of George Michael and Andrew Ridgeley with their Club Tropicana tans, and think it shows something quite defiantly anti-cool and suburban about them. I didn't know it at the time, but my love of a tan was revealing about me and where

I came from, as were many of my conventional values and judgements.

27 May – *'Weather was gorgeous today, I was really annoyed at having to go to work. Sunbathed for a while when I got home though. In the evening Deb, Hannah, Gill and Tim went out for a meal, I didn't go cos I don't like Greek food. Saw* Kojak.'

In August, we went on holiday to Spain for a fortnight, flying from the archetypally suburban Luton airport. It was only my second time ever abroad, and after a seventeen-hour delay caused by a strike, we flew off to a villa with a small, not particularly picturesque swimming pool, overlooking a scrubby dry landscape. I sunbathed myself to a crisp, and ate English food every single day, making sure to record the unvarying menu – *'steak and chips . . . chicken and chips . . . ice cream and chocolate sauce . . . fried breakfast as usual . . . steak and chips . . . chicken and chips . . . fish and chips . . . pork chops . . . ice cream . . . chicken and chips . . . turkey steaks . . . fish and chips . . .'* When we got back home, we had fish and chips for dinner, to celebrate.

17 August – *'Everyone at the shops said how brown we look!'* but next day, *'Saw Huw. He was rude about my tan.'* Someone knew what the rules were.

What most excited me was music and boys, ideally at the same time. On May the 29th, I went to see Ian Dury at Hemel Hempstead Pavilion. He had broken his leg, and couldn't play, so the support bands played, and the gig was rescheduled. '*Met a bloke called Steve. He bought me a drink, then we had a natter, went and sat down in the balcony, and I got off with him. He's really gorgeous.*'

30 May – '*I still keep thinking about Steve. He lives in Harpenden, wears plastic trousers, doesn't like TRB (Tom Robinson Band), has got short brown curly hair, is quite tall and skinny. I sunbathed quite a lot today. Getting really brown. Steve was pretty brown too. There I go again.*'

I was fifteen years old now, and in common with all my friends I knew something and nothing about sex. The pamphlet Mum gave me at home was followed up by some rudimentary lessons at school.

8 March – '*Double biology was quite interesting today – human reproduction!!*'

20 March – '*Mrs Thomas was being crude in biology again – going on about her personal experiences!!*' And one week our PE teacher stood in to take the biology lesson, talking about sex and ending the lesson with, 'Next week I'll tell you what it FEELS like!' before swishing out of the room, leaving behind a silence in the air which had frozen around our astonished, gaping little faces. Other than these lessons, we had nowhere to go for information, no one to ask, except each other, and we were hardly reliable.

There is nothing nowadays to compare with this level of ignorance, and most teens get proper education at school, at home and online, sharing facts and knowledge, googling anything they may need to know. Our beliefs were informed by reading the Cathy and Claire page in *Jackie* magazine, and our contraceptive experience was limited to condoms, which we called Durex or Rubber Johnnies, and only a couple of girls were on the pill. We had a sense of utter doom about pregnancy, it being so dreaded and taboo that we had somehow absorbed the message that condoms ALWAYS broke, and we were filled with the conviction that pregnancy was the inevitable consequence of any sexual contact at all.

Between ourselves we tried to come up with a way of talking about something we didn't understand and had almost no experience of.

12 June – *'We have got a code to measure how far you go with people. Base 1 = French kiss. 1½ = Outside upstairs. Base 2 = Inside upstairs. 2½ = Outside (clothes, that is) downstairs. Base 3 = Inside downstairs. 3½ = 69 etc. Base 4 = All the way. I got to about Base 2½ with Steve.'*

I love the idea that we included '69' in our list, as if that was the kind of sex any of us were having. And I'm almost impressed at myself for having got anywhere at all in the balcony at a gig.

On June the 13th I was talking on the phone to a friend. *'We discussed BASES. B has got to Base 3½ I think. I've only got to Base 3! Ah well. A has got to 3 too. Saw Rhoda and went to bed at 10.'*

15 June – the date of the rescheduled Ian Dury gig: '*Steve was there. I spoke to him for a while but J got off with him. Got loads of badges and a poster. It was just like a big party really.*'

16 June – '*J is going out with Steve, I think. I wasn't REALLY that annoyed when she got off with him last nite cos I find him a bit conceited and chauvinistic. I LOVE THE BLOCKHEADS.*'

This was an outright lie: I was gutted about not getting off with Steve again, but too proud to admit it, even to my supposedly private diary. Honestly, I sometimes think this diary was no friend to me at all. I couldn't tell it anything. I was briefly bullied at school around this time. Classic girl-bullying; nothing physical, no pushing or shoving, just whispers, a comment passed here and there. I didn't quite catch it, and then I did, presumably because I was meant to. And it was viciously personal, leaving me with a specific physical anxiety that haunted me for years. But in my diary? Nothing. Not a word. I was the most unreliable narrator of all time. I've said before that there is an element of control involved in this, and that's true, but there's also denial. An attempt to make events vanish or unhappen by not writing about them, which is a kind of magical thinking, and perhaps less helpful. Years later a therapist would have to do all the detective work of uncovering the words I hadn't said, which I had hoped I had forgotten, but which instead wrote themselves on my brain instead of the page.

I didn't dare, I just didn't dare. Writing things down was terrifying, made them real. Instead, I retreated into books and records. I read *The Exorcist*, and *Catch 22*: '*a brilliant book, really funny*'.

23 June – '*Mum and Dad played golf in the evening and Deb played tennis. Me, I just played records.*'

9 July – '*Saw* The London Weekend Show – *it was absolutely fantastic, an interview with Bowie, clips of him onstage, chats with the fans etc. Bowie looked gorgeous. He was brilliant onstage. Listened to Annie Nightingale. I taped Bruce Springsteen "Racing in the Streets" last night so I've been listening to that all day. I love it.*'

I'd made friends with an older boy called Huw, who had a fanzine called the *Weekly Bugle*.

17 July – '*Borrowed* Heroes *album. It's really good. Wrote a letter to the* Weekly Bugle *about the general lack of entertainment in Hertfordshire.*'

Out there, somewhere, things were happening, and there were people in the world like David Bowie, and Annie Nightingale, and Bruce Springsteen. But not here, not now.

Like so many girls before me, I encountered music partly via older boys, seeing the light of rock and roll refracted through their prism, catching the sound waves that bounced off them. Huw was one, and my brother Keith, ten years older than me, was another. Huw knew about Suicide, and Keith had gritty records by The Faces, but when I made the move from pop and disco into new record buying, I started with the romantic end of punk, energetic love songs rather than shouty slogans: the first Undertones album, Elvis Costello's *My Aim is True*, The Cure's *Three Imaginary Boys* and Buzzcocks' *Another Music in a Different Kitchen*. Along with these, and perhaps slightly out of place, sat Springsteen's *Darkness on the Edge of Town*, which I bought when it came out in 1978.

I'm not certain how I came to buy that record. Possibly because he'd co-written Patti Smith's 'Because the Night', and she was an early heroine. But also possibly because on the cover was a photo of him wearing a leather jacket, looking just punk enough, and very much like a young Al Pacino. On the whole British punks didn't look like Al Pacino. And although I was a mixed-up girl who spent days listening to the Raincoats and doing my homework inside the wardrobe, that was only half the time. The other half, in truth, I spent gazing at the cover of *Darkness on the Edge of Town*, in a way that I never gazed at the cover of *My Aim Is True*.

I also liked the record inside, despite its exotic otherness. On the surface his songs were all about cars and badlands and mean streets and stuff I knew nothing about, but underneath they were all about desperate yearning and thwarted desire, and at sixteen I was full of both of those. Bruce sounded like he'd listened to Lou Reed, and Spector, and The Shangri-Las' tumultuous street ballads. And above all he fitted into my instinctive love for the romantic underdog. Emotional lyrics about heroic losers. Songs that reached straight for your heart. I fell a little bit in love with Springsteen, and wondered why you never seemed to meet a Real Boy who looked like that or who'd write passionate songs about you. And maybe even have a car.

And then, of course, there was David Bowie, who entered my life not via an underground record shop, or the *NME*, but by hearing him on Radio One and seeing him on *Top of the Pops*, and playing Keith's copy of *Ziggy Stardust*, which had been lying around the house since I was a child. He embedded himself in my consciousness primarily as a pop artist, a writer of songs so packed full of hooks you were caught on first listen. I loved the Ziggy album because it was strange and yet familiar, and I could sing along with all of it. In 1978, I went to see The Human League at the Nashville and wrote, '*Plain Characters were on first, morons chucked glasses and crates at them. Human League were fantastic. There was a lot of trouble though. Thought we were gonna get beaten up. I'm convinced David Bowie walked past me – I nearly died of shock.'* It was the closest I'd ever be to him. But like many people, I felt he was always there.

When he died, the one thing I thought wasn't emphasised enough in all the tributes and obituaries was the simple fact that none of the art/image/gender stuff would have had as much impact without the tunes, such phenomenal tunes. If you'd never heard Bowie, many descriptions make his work sound arch, cool and detached. But he'd been part of the pre-ironic period of pop, not afraid of sincerity, especially in his singing, and through all the tributes and memories, what became clear was that everyone had some personal recollection that encapsulated his meaning for them. My little story is one I've told before, in *Bedsit Disco Queen*, of the day when I was rehearsing in someone's bedroom with my first band Stern Bops, and on being asked to sing, replied that I couldn't do it if they were all looking at me. Instead I got into the wardrobe and, once inside the stuffy darkness, out of sight but clutching my microphone, sang 'Rebel Rebel'. It was my first ever vocal performance.

How hilarious, you might think, how pitiful even, to sing an anthem to rebelliousness while hiding in a closet. How could you take all the defiance and pride of that song, and undermine it with fear? But the more I think about it, the more I realise that this is exactly how inspirational artists work, and why we need them. They don't inspire the brave (they're fine already); they inspire the timid.

I'm thinking again about that idea that art flourishes in an unconducive environment, that suburbia is inspiring, surrounding you with ideas and people to reject. For David Bowie, and the Bromley punks, that's clearly true, but I don't know whether or not it applies to me, whether it was a spur or a hindrance, whether it inhibited me as much as it prompted. In different surroundings, maybe I'd have been braver, made more noise, pushed a little further? I was naturally shy, but I was also unconfrontational, with none of the innate courage that allows someone to stroll round a quiet suburb dressed like an alien. Those kinds of people are the trailblazers, the ones who light the way. I loved their look, but I wouldn't have been able to endure the looks. Although, I didn't know they were suburban; I just assumed they all lived in Soho, or Chelsea, and that David Bowie had fallen to earth from another planet. If I'd known they all went to school in Bromley, might it have helped?

Still, you don't copy people you're inspired by. Quite often you can't; you wouldn't know where to start. You can only stare, open-mouthed in wonder. And yet still something happens, you hear a voice telling you something; a little tiny spark is lit. And you treasure that spark, and add it to others that you're finding elsewhere, gathering them around you like a protective halo. Until you have just enough courage to take that song you love to dance to and sing those words you love to sing. Even from inside a wardrobe.

1978

From the middle of the year onwards, my overwhelming emotion was boredom. Frustration intensified. I talked to a school friend about '*starting our own music paper*', and wrote that '*work was incredibly dull. Everyone at that supermarket is getting on my nerves. I AM FED UP.*' Next day: '*I AM STILL FED UP.*' And the mood continued.

26 August 1978 – '*Work again. I was bored out of my mind.*'

5 September – '*I was so bored at school today. I've realised I hate it.*'

7 September – '*School was a bore today.*'

11 September – '*I was bored today at school.*'

20 September – '*School was really dull today.*'

18 November – '*Work was boring and irritating. I didn't have anywhere to go so I stayed in and had a bath and got bored and depressed. God, this diary's getting boring. Can't be bothered to write*

any more' – and the entry finished halfway down the page, which was unusual.

22 November – *'Went to a careers talk, some bloke from St Albans talking about secretarial courses, very dull indeed.'*

The boredom grew, and solidified, like an iceberg, threatening to scupper me. It was both real and fake, partly true and partly a punk pose. In order to counter the tedium, we often turned to booze. There were no age checks or ID issues, and not much concern about drinking and driving. It was a rural/suburban thing, the acceptance that everyone went to the pub, as there was nowhere else to go. Nowadays teens buy their own booze and drink it at home or in the park. But we were a different generation. We didn't buy cheap supermarket vodka and pre-load in our bedrooms before going out. Instead, we went to the same pubs as all the older people, and no one stopped us or asked us or noticed us.

And we drank note-perfect 1970s drinks, strange, vivid syrupy mixtures: gin with undiluted orange squash, lager with lime cordial, vodka with grenadine, the colour and flavour of the rinse-and-spit mouthwash at the dentist's.

13 May 1977 – *'Went round to the off-licence and bought some booze to take to the party tomorrow – 4 bottles of Babycham and 2 bottles of Moussec.'*

31 October – At a Halloween disco in Potters Bar, *'All the booze was free, we were drinking straight Martinis.'*

We went on pub crawls around the local villages. On one occasion I recorded three different pubs in three different villages being visited, *'got slightly smashed'* (I was still only fifteen), and the following day: *'Felt really ill all day at work. Slightly hungover to say the least.'*

2 June – At the Two Brewers: *'Had a few gins and got a little drunk.'*

22 August – Again, at a party in Hatfield: *'Drank about half a bottle Martini and half bottle Cinzano and got pissed out of my mind. Was sick at the party. Came home about 12 and was sick again. Collapsed into bed.'*

24 September – And again, at the Hope and Anchor in Welham Green: *'Everyone bought us loads of drinks, I had about 11 Cinzanos!! We were all really smashed. P looked a bit ill, he had to go outside for a walk.'*

There was very little in the way of drugs on offer, but we smoked dope; my first time being another example of evasiveness in my diary:

22 September – *'Huw is leaving home soon and moving to London. Went back to his house for coffee + !!*!??!!*!'* What that means is that I smoked a joint for the first time, but like the day of the completely blank page, I don't actually say what had happened or describe it in any way. It had been slightly embarrassing. The joint made me feel sick, and made me burp, but I wasn't going to write that down.

On another date, I was slightly less evasive, writing, '*Got absolutely stoned and went back to Huw's for coffee. He showed me all his art stuff and gave me some photos*.' Mum always misused the word 'stoned' to mean 'drunk', so I may have thought this was safe enough to write. But this makes me laugh: I drank booze, and occasionally took drugs, but I didn't drink coffee.

28 May – '*Went back to Huw's for coffee. Well, I had orange squash!!*' That strange note of unsophistication continued even when I first got to university. When we'd gather in someone's student flat for late-night coffee, I'd have a glass of milk, and sometimes they would take the piss out of the way I pronounced milk in my Hatfield accent, with a 'w' sound where the 'l' should be.

Along with the occasional joint, we took stimulating cough tablets containing ephedrine, or our mothers' sleeping tablets or tranquillisers. At school on October the 3rd, '*Had my polio booster. They asked me if I took any tablets or anything (!!*!!) so I just said Piritons. Ho ho.*'

24 November – At a party in Brookmans Park, I took speed tablets, '*didn't sleep a wink all night*'. The next day, '*didn't go to work cos I felt so sick and ill and tired*'. None of this could cure the boredom. It took the edge off slightly, but it wasn't enough. And whatever we drank or took, we'd jump in a car afterwards to get home, and there'd be crashes.

10 August 1977 – '*JL drove his car into a lamp post – NB and AG were in it – they're alright though.*'

21 November 1979 – '*Huw crashed his car a few weeks ago – it's a write-off and he's got 3 broken ribs.*'

One evening in 1978 a group of us went to a disco, then to the pub, and then, '*on the way home we went to see the crash down Bluebridge Rd*'. What perfect suburban entertainment, to go and look at the wreckage as the highlight of a Saturday night. The car had been full of people we knew and had crashed the night before. '*There were nine people in the car including P and A. It skidded and turned over. A gashed all his leg and P went back to the Waters's house to clean up etc.*'

Nine people in that car. It must have seemed like fun until it wasn't.

1978

On September the 26th I turned sixteen, still two years away from being legal in pubs. Debbie bought me Patti Smith's *Horses*, someone else lent me Lou Reed's *Transformer*. '*I don't feel any different than when I was 15. Oh well. 16 sounds better though.*'

Gigs and sex, gigs and violence.

30 September – It was Ultravox at St Albans City Hall, and I got off with a boy called Steve: '*We all went outside, me and Steve went behind the Civic. WHT! Really randy. He has got 3 earrings in one ear. They walked us home. Sat in the precinct for a while.*'

11 October – I went to see Siouxsie and the Banshees, '*Bloke claiming to be from* Melody Maker *wanted to take my pic. Slapped my bum too.*' I didn't seem to mind. But on November the 6th, we went to see Buzzcocks and Subway Sect at Hemel Hempstead, and afterwards: '*Went to the Chinese with Jon and Russell. Got molested by gang of morons. Really frightening. Morons followed us home. Russell cried.*'

And through it all I carried on lying to myself via the medium of my diary.

1 December – I went to a disco in St Albans. The boy I'd arranged to meet there ignored me and went off with someone else. '*I got so depressed cos no one seemed to like me. Everyone had gone off and left me. M came back and cheered me up. He was lovely. Told me he loved me and kissed me. I cheered up. Later on M mauled me (I don't mind!) The other M kissed me goodbye. Still a bit depressed though.*' The boy who'd ignored me phoned me up next day to apologise, so I met up with him again, but I could tell he wasn't really interested, and so next day:

3 December – '*I've decided I don't like him any more. He's really rather boring. I mean, he's a nice enough bloke, but nothing out-standing. So that's that as far as I'm concerned.*' I found out next day he was going to a party with someone else. '*I'm relieved cos I don't like him any more, but still a bit narked that he'll be there.*' This, of course, wasn't true. I DID like him. Secrets and lies. Secrets and lies.

Anyway, I went to the party, he was there, and so I got off with his friend instead. '*M got pissed and was thrown out so I stayed outside with him. Had to keep walking round the car park with him to sober him up. D was disapproving cos I was stoned again.*'

I can't tell now, looking back from this distance, whether I was having fun or not. I sound pretty fed up, partly putting on a brave face and partly getting out of my head whenever I could. Which probably was fun, at least some of the time. And there was still Christmas to enjoy. '*Got up about 8.30 and opened presents. I got a pair of shoes,* Penetration *LP, talc, perfume, earrings. Christmas dinner was lovely. Turkey, loads of booze. Watched a bit of* The Sound of Music, *it was hilarious. Saw* Battle for the Planet of the Apes, *and* Morecambe and Wise. *Played cards. Kept eating nearly all day (and drinking!!).*'

The year ended with me sitting at home. There was thick snow, Debbie went off to a disco in Brent, '*I didn't have anywhere to go so I had to sit at home on New Year's Eve and watch TV. God, how depressing. Part 2 of* The Old Grey Whistle Test *with Patti Smith, the Tubes, Vibrators, Blondie, Magazine, Elvis Costello. Said hello to 79 and went to bed.*'

I'm not the only person to have grown up stifled and bored in suburbia; it's almost the law. The diary entries, this monotonous litany of having nothing to do, are a relentless howl of frustrated energy. Brookmans Park was stultifying, frozen in time. In the world at large, things changed a lot during the 1960s and '70s, but in the heart of the Green Belt nothing seemed to move. Stranded in the past, it wrestled with the present, and hated the future. And there I was, stuck with it.

Now, when I read the history of the place, and look at the statistics, I can see what had happened. The original plan for Brookmans Park was for it to increase ultimately to a population of 7,500, but in fact it never got above 3,530. The population of the parish of North Mymms, which includes Brookmans Park and the neighbouring villages of Welham Green and Bell Bar, had grown steadily for 200 years, then came to a sudden and complete halt. In 1801 the parish population was 838. By 1931 it had grown to 3,015, and by 1951 it was 5,526, and by 1961 – 12,522. And there it stopped. In 1971 the population was still only 12,405, and ten years later, still the same. I was born in 1962, the exact moment when the place stopped growing. From that point there was no building, no expansion, no immigration, no emigration. No change.

The creation of the Green Belt resulted in a pushing up of house prices, and as time went by Brookmans Park became increasingly anachronistic and uncharacteristic. Fifty-nine per cent of the houses now are detached, which is double the national average. Twenty-one per cent of the houses have 5+ bedrooms, which is FOUR TIMES the national average. The place is an exclusive garden village rather than a suburb, with an older population than England as a whole, and a higher percentage of married couples. A recent survey of residents asked the question 'Main place of work?' and the answers, in order, were – 1. Retired. 2. London 3. Home.

One other factor that inhibited the development of Brookmans Park was the presence of its most significant building, and one we all drove past regularly without paying it any attention: the Transmitting Station, which sits on the A1000 between Potters Bar and Hatfield, or the Great North Road as we called it. Built in 1929 it was a groundbreaking twin transmitter, able to broadcast two radio programmes at the same time. Before this, only one programme at a time could be transmitted, and reception was often poor, or non-existent, beyond a radius of about three miles. The Brookmans Park station, ironically, was known as the London station, and was part of a plan to extend coverage across the country, beginning with London and the Home Counties.

The site – set 440 feet above sea level, one of the highest

points in Hertfordshire (in the Domesday Reloaded documents, it is described as being 'the highest point of land between York and Russia'), and only fifteen miles from central London – was bought by the BBC from the Brookmans Park Estate for £10,000, during the slump in housing sales at the end of the 1920s. After the purchase, the BBC then insisted that any further lots sold by the Estate imposed restrictions on the buyer, preventing the use of machinery or apparatus that could interfere with the Broadcasting Station. This covenant, along with the Green Belt restrictions of 1947, further prevented Brookmans Park developing as anything other than a residential village. There could be a wireless shop, and a hairdresser, but no heavy industry.

Given how disparaging I've been about the blandness of all the local buildings, it's also salutary to note that, because of the absence of much in the way of planning restrictions at the time, the designers and builders of the station were allowed to do more or less what they liked. BBC engineer P.P. Eckersley, a key player in the Regional Scheme that extended coverage, wrote in 1941: 'A high-power wireless station is such a lovely thing. The process is silent, there is no gas or smell or fussy reciprocation, no sound except a purposeful humming. One is conscious of power contained and controlled. I felt that the building should be fitting to performance.'

He had the support of Sir John Reith, head of the BBC, in this plan, and the new transmitting stations were made larger than they strictly needed to be, in order to symbolise the status of broadcasting, and its significant role in national life. And so the new station at Brookmans Park measured 20,500 square feet, replacing a transmitter that had been only 725 square feet in size.

I can't help thinking now of the presence of this building, which I knew almost nothing about, and to which I paid no attention. I felt remote and isolated and yet, there it was, so nearby, increasing radio receptivity and enhancing the possibilities of broadcasting, of connectivity. I picture myself in my bedroom, feeling solitary and disconnected, stranded on a kind of desert island bereft of culture, perhaps listening to the John Peel show, which felt like it was being beamed to me from a distant star, and yet was actually reaching my bedroom via a signal from the station just a mile up the road.

Or I might have been playing my seven-inch single of Joy Division's 'Transmission'.

Radio, live transmission. Radio, live transmission.

All those lyrics would have resonated so strongly with me.

Listen to the silence, let it ring on.
And we would go on as though nothing was wrong . . .
Staying in the same place . . .

I imagine the song building to its crescendo, and those final lines, 'Dance, dance, dance, dance, dance to the radio', repeating again and again, and perhaps I was doing just that, dancing and dancing, in the secrecy of my lonely room, while up the hill, in the silence and darkness of the field in which it stood, the transmitting station went about its quiet business, purposefully humming.

I ask myself sometimes, was it harder to be a girl than a boy in 1970s suburbia? I can only imagine it was. The conventionality, the strictness of the rules, meant you stood out far too easily if you didn't exactly fit the mould. The only examples I saw around me were that men went up to London to work every day, while women were mothers and housewives, or did part-time jobs: typing, or serving in a shop, like my mum. There was not much sign of 1970s feminism in Brookmans Park. In a nod to changing fashion, Mum bought a midi-skirt and some tight boots, which she never wore, and there were jokes about bra-burning and Women's Lib, but it was considered disloyal to criticise husbands, so there was not much sense of female solidarity, which might have provided comfort, or an opportunity for expressing frustration.

By the age of sixteen I was thoroughly dissatisfied with where I found myself and was embarking on a reinvention. But there was conflict involved in all of this, and a lot of secrecy, which seemed part of the very fabric of suburbia. All utopias contain the seeds of their opposite, and Brookmans Park was so picture perfect, it was unreal, like a *Truman Show* stage set. My teenage feelings of awkwardness and self-consciousness were amplified by the fact that any tiny deviation stood out like a sore thumb, any whisper would be heard as a scream. And I was too timid to actually scream.

I was in need of role models, but in that place at that time they were few and far between. Diary entries from 1978 show that I was starting to notice them:

14 September 1978 – '*Did some painting in the evening. I painted a picture of Patti Smith.*'

21 January 1979 – '*Watched* The London Weekend Show. *It was all about women in the music biz. Siouxsie Sioux and Rachel Sweet were on it. It was quite interesting.*'

22 January – '*Saw a prog called* Who is Poly Styrene? *It was all about her and the band. Clips of them live, in the studio etc. It was a really good film.*'

And in 1979, I went to a gig at the Moonlight Club in West Hampstead, excitedly writing: '*First on were the Glass Torpedoes and they were really excellent. Then Swell Maps came on and I enjoyed them too. Moonlight Club is v small, good atmosphere. Saw all the Raincoats down there – they were sitting next to us!!*'

Out there in the big wide world beyond my bedroom there were women getting to work who were less afraid, and who were going to help change my life and liberate me, and I would owe so much to them, as they'd open up a world of possibility. I wouldn't realise quite how much I owed them all until much later. I would buy records by them and their bands, and see them play live, but not until a flurry of books were published around 2014 did I fully piece together their stories, and also begin to realise how much they changed things.

In 1976, aged twenty-one, Viv Albertine inherited two hundred quid from her grandmother and bought an electric guitar. Already a member of punk's inner circle – the girlfriend of Mick Jones, the best friend of Sid Vicious – this was nonetheless an audacious act, and as she would write decades later in her book, *Clothes Music Boys*: 'Who'd done it before me? There was no one I could identify with. No girls played electric guitar. Especially not ordinary girls like me.' She was speaking for me, and so many like me.

With that guitar she joined Ari Up, Tessa Pollitt and Palmolive in The Slits. Eschewing the generic garage-band sound of their punk contemporaries, they incorporated reggae and soul into their sound – Viv says she wanted her guitar to sound like the chops on Dionne Warwick records – and invented post-punk before anyone else had even tired of punk. With their back-combed hair, dreads, tutus, ripped tights and Doc Martens, they were the most anarchic and badly behaved band on the White Riot tour with the Clash, Buzzcocks and Subway Sect, and it was they who were thrown out of hotels, for making a racket and pissing in people's shoes in the corridors.

In her book, she conveyed brilliantly the sheer rebellious glee of being in a band when you don't really know what you're doing, the childish pleasure of the onstage fuck-you attitude they embodied. Not knowing that the chant 'One-two-three-four' is supposed to set the speed of the song, she'd simply assumed that it was 'a warning to the band that you're starting and it's to be shouted as fast as possible, the quicker, the more exciting.' I understood that so clearly. I remembered being a teenage music fan, and being as excited by music and its possibilities as the boys were, but still somehow feeling shut out. The boys seemed to know, or to invent, so many of its rules, so many of its values. There were apparent facts and bits of knowledge that we didn't understand, or perhaps were deliberately kept from knowing. Sometimes, being a girl in a band, or a female music fan, you felt like you'd missed a meeting, like they'd turned up an hour before you and stuck a 'No Girls' sign on the door.

When I formed a band I thought of The Slits as our scary big sisters, but they were inspirational nonetheless. All of us were trapped in such an awkward spot, and at that time, rock was such a hard place. Not long after Viv Albertine, Chrissie Hynde also wrote a memoir, *Reckless*, and controversy swirled around her apparent blaming of herself for a sexual assault she suffered as a teen. The whole sad story reminded me again what it used to mean to be a rock fan and a rebel in the 1960s and 1970s. Chrissie told her tale in a style of swaggering bravado, eulogising her male rock heroes – 'I wanted to be them, not do them' – and the biker gangs she idolised – 'I loved the bikes and I loved the way they talked about honour and loyalty and brotherhood', but then had to squirm through a line of questioning that accused her of having the wrong attitude to her rape. Hang on, she objected, I never used the word rape. And it's true, she never did, instead describing the actual assault in a tone that implied she regarded it more as some kind of awful initiation. Getting what she calls her 'comeuppance', she said it was her fault for failing the code, for being too mouthy. All she wanted, it seems, was to be respected by the bad guys, to be admitted to their ranks.

This, understandably, didn't go down well, and she was accused of victim blaming. But her plight seemed to me very much the plight of a female rock fan of her age. Born in 1951, she had no female role models. To be a woman meant to have no place in the rock scene she adored, and so, she wrote, 'I thought sex was, like becoming "a woman", something to put off for as long as possible.' Desperate to be one of the guys, she accepted their rules – no complaining, no whining, taking it like a man. Hence her macho stance of refusing to blame anyone but herself.

But in those few years at the end of the '70s, Viv, along with Patti and Ari, and Siouxsie and Poly and Chrissie, made more progress for women in music than we could have imagined. I think about how different things were for the generations who followed. By the time Carrie Brownstein came to form her band Sleater-Kinney, springing from the Olympia, Washington, punk and indie scene of the early '90s, so much had changed. Chrissie Hynde had acted as an individual, an outrider. She grew up going to see The Stones, The Who and Led Zeppelin, and as for women at that time, she said, 'you could count them on one hand'. But Carrie Brownstein was born in

1974, her first gig was Madonna, and by the mid-'90s she had the whole Riot Grrrl scene to call on – 'a network of people finding their voices' – and both the participants and the subject matter had changed – in her book *Hunger Makes Me a Modern Girl*, she wrote: 'Girls wrote and sang about sexism and sexual assault, about shitty bosses and boyfriends.' Feminism and gender politics had reasserted themselves, and this time the girls in music weren't playing second fiddle.

I remember going to a Riot Grrrl gig in London in the early '90s, where the bands were Huggy Bear and Bikini Kill, and the audience was women only, unlike the days of punk, when there may have been women onstage but men usually ruled the room. At other gigs, Kathleen Hanna from Bikini Kill would yell from the stage – 'All girls to the front. I'm not kidding. All girls to the front. All boys be cool for once in your lives. Go back. Back!' and she'd wave the guys out of the mosh-pit and towards the back of the club, finally laying claim to a literal space for women to inhabit. It would feel like the culmination of a years-long rebuttal of the rules of rock and roll.

So it's easy to forget that once upon a time the only available identity was male. Even Patti Smith, our heroine and champion for so long now, wrote about seeing Keith Richard and wanting to BE him. In the words of that great feminist saying, quoted by Caitlin Moran – 'I cannot be what I cannot see', but there was a generation of women who took that fact and turned it on its head. They wanted to be just like the guys – and sometimes that came at painful expense to themselves – but in doing so they opened up the options for female identity. And those of us who followed – we could be something new, because we could see them.

All of these women were out there. All this would happen. All this would come. But for now I was still waiting and hoping. Listening for signals. Scanning the horizon, squinting into the far distance, hoping for something new.

1979

A red Collins pocket diary, one page per day. Inside is a tube map, an Intercity rail map, a list of bank holidays, weights and measures, sunrise and sunset times, a metric conversion table and three pages of first aid.

'Bone, broken or dislocated – Send for doctor at once and do not touch or attempt to move limb. Poisoning – If someone is thought to have swallowed poison, telephone a doctor for advice, even if no effects have appeared. Burns and scalds – if clothing is on fire smother flame and rip off smouldering clothing.'

Inside the diary, I was still recording things that didn't happen.

2 January 1979 – *'Went up to London with Deb. We walked right up and down Oxford St and I only bought a pair of socks. Then we went over to Knightsbridge and went to Harrods. Debbie didn't buy anything either.'*

I was still listing everything I saw on the telly, which now included *The Bionic Woman*, *Robin's Nest*, *The Kenny Everett Video Show* and *Agony*.

1 April – I saw *'Part 1 of* King, *series of 3 programmes about Martin Luther King, really good.'*

2 April – *'Saw part 2 of* King.'

3 April – *'Watched last part of* King. *He got shot tonight and died. Really sad. The programme was brilliant though.'*

I wonder if I knew he was going to get shot? I'm honestly not sure I did.

I was reading *Coma*, *The Eyes of Laura Mars* and *Valley of the Dolls*.

17 February – I was dancing at a party to *'some good records – 'Heart of Glass', 'Shame', 'Rhythm Stick', 'White Punks On Dope', 'Jean Genie', 'Mighty Real'.'*

And the year began with snow again, adding to all our usual transport difficulties. On January the 9th I was trying to get to St Albans with Huw to a gig. First we planned to go on the train, but there was a train strike – *'We've gotta go on the bus cos he's got no petrol'* – so we ended up getting a bus to South Mymms, then another bus to St Albans, coming home via a bus BACK to South Mymms and then a three-mile walk through ice and snow to Huw's house, from where I finally got a lift home.

Suburban transport was such a big deal. My sister learned to drive as soon as she could, but my teens would pass without me ever wanting to, although I would then be persuaded in my late twenties, when after two or three (tellingly, I have forgotten) driving tests I would be deemed competent, aware that only I knew the truth, which was that I had no idea what I was doing. Erratic, indecisive and directionless, I drove with all the skill and consistency of a drunk on the dodgems. During my year behind the wheel I kept pointing this out to people, only to be met with wry chuckles, murmurs of 'Pfft, don't be so modest, ANYONE can drive' and assertions that any kinks in my technique would soon be ironed out with practice. So I kept practising, feeling that I must be mistaken in believing that I was an accident waiting to happen. Until the moment when the accident stopped waiting, and happened, and I drove into someone.

I have forgotten many things about my driving. I can't even recall whether my instructor was a man or a woman, which speaks to me of some fairly efficient and deliberate memory cleansing. One of the security questions my bank likes to ask me is, 'What was your first car?', and as it was my ONLY car you'd think the answer would spring to mind quickly. In fact I have blotted that out too, and the information hides quivering somewhere behind a mental sofa. But the one thing I do remember, from The Year of Driving Dangerously, is the crashing. You're probably picturing me tootling along at forty on the motorway, or being overtaken by milk floats on residential roads – a nuisance to all but a danger to nobody. I'll set you straight on that one. Nervous drivers don't drive too slow, they drive too fast. Like those who drink too quickly at the start of a party to calm the jitters, I would put my foot down in order to get the whole thing over with. Combined with an inability to judge distance or speed, and a desperate desire not to be a bore at junctions and roundabouts, my fear made me a menace, and when I finally crashed it was the sheer inevitability of it that wounded me. Luckily the accident was not fatal, or even injurious, but it was final, an absolute bitter end.

When Debbie had learned to drive at seventeen, we immediately became very reliant on her little second-hand Fiat.

16 January – *'Bad news, Deb's car has broken down – how will we get about this weekend aaarrgghh.'*

23 January – *'It snowed really hard all night and most of today. Coach turned up about 9. Finally started our exam at 10. They sent us all home at 1 cos the weather was getting so bad. Also there was loads of traffic cos all the trains are on strike.'*

Boredom continued to be the theme of my narrative, bringing out in me a mean, judgemental streak.

26 January –*'Went to the Two Brewers. We saw P and J there. They were their usual boring selves. P came out with his usual comments – How's life? How's school? Bought any records lately?'*

12 March – *'Saw P who has slicked his hair down and gone NORMAL. So have N and J etc. God, what's come over them all? BOORING.'*

This mean streak extended into a startling lack of sympathy shown towards anyone who owned up to difficult or complicated feelings. For instance, this casual entry in January about a friend of a friend, '*He's really depressed cos his dad's died and he's tried to commit suicide 3 times*', and this one concerning two separate friends, '*S has chucked A. He's gone really weird lately and has started talking about suicide. I hope he's gonna be alright. B is still away. Me and A keep taking the piss out of all her depression lark. She's really beginning to annoy us.*' I'd mentioned B's depression before, and was rigid and harsh in my dismissal of her, '*I phoned B. She had a nice holiday but is still depressed. Stupid girl. She sounds like something off a Cathy and Claire problem page.*' And in March, '*B was away today cos she went to the psychiatrist (POSEUR).*' I can only conclude now that these things frightened me, that talking about feelings was verboten, and that she was breaking the code by opening up, seeking help. Brave and progressive of her considering the prevailing mood of the time, the way we took the piss out of everything, and the peculiar medical information we all absorbed – on another occasion I wrote, '*B was away. She came out in a rash and when she went to the doctor he told her she's allergic to beefburgers.*'

I had clearly come to the conclusion that B was just showing off, as that was what I had been taught. I can't help but contrast this attitude of mine, and the general tone of secrecy and silence surrounding such issues as depression, suicide, mental health, with the current move towards openness. As I write this, members of the Royal Family (Princes William and Harry) are on TV talking about their mental health struggles and supporting others to seek help. At the same time, I get an email from my son's school, alerting parents to a couple of matters which 'have arisen that cause us a degree of concern'. And these are, firstly, the Netflix series *13 Reasons Why*, which seems to suggest that suicide is a reasonable response to certain pressures, and secondly a new social-media challenge called the 'Blue Whale Challenge', which sets kids tasks, and includes them carving the shape of a blue whale on their hand, the final one being suicide. The letter attaches links to two helpful articles about both these issues, and ends by saying 'As you would imagine we will be discussing these issues at school in the days ahead but you will understand our need to share this information with you so that you are as informed as you can be as well.'

This is progress, isn't it, pure and simple. Back in 1979 such things were shrouded in darkness, and if by any chance you were forced to confront them, the correct response was to make a joke of it all and revert to the safety of comedy.

2 April – '*B moaned about her illnesses all day. Scandal – K had a party on Saturday at which S ended up having it off with P's bloke in the potting shed. P's really upset. General hysteria etc. Nasty atmosphere at school. Saw Kenny Everett.*'

1979

The stories you tell about your past try to impose some kind of order upon it, force it to make sense, and fit you into other narratives of the time. I've looked at these diaries before, and written some of this story before, and part of what I did was to try to make it sound cool. Like all there was to do was form a band, and so that was all I did. Tidying, tidying. Editing, editing. There's so much else that didn't fit, so many jarring juxtapositions; the yoking together of the mundane and the exciting, the urban and suburban, the naff and the cool. My life now was such a mixture of smooth and spiky, of convention and rejection of convention.

13 January – *'Bought Elvis Costello's "Armed Forces" and Subway Sect's "Ambition". Mum and dad got me a cassette case with their Green Shield stamps.'*

5 March – *'Woke up about 9. Gave Mum a plant for Mother's Day. Weather was really lovely today. Deb went to choir practice. In the afternoon we went jogging. Played our TRB tapes – they're brilliant. Taped Sham 69 and Devo. Really great. Did some English*

114

and history homework. Did my room. Washed hair. Me, Mum and Dad played cards for a while in the evening. Heard XTC "All Along The Watchtower". I love that record it's fantastic.'

It's true that I was going to gigs and trying to be cool, but I was also still going to discos in suburban cricket clubs. Because of this, I began to be anxious and acutely self-aware. There are diary entries that scornfully describe scenes straight out of *Abigail's Party*.

28 January – *'We had to go up to the L's at 12 for lunchtime drinks, god how pretentious.'*

23 June – *'Mum and Dad went up to the golf club in the evening for a Caribbean evening.'* (I don't even want to think about that one.)

21 July – *'In the evening the C's came for a fondue party with Mum and Dad.'*

Meanwhile I tried to turn myself into the opposite of all this – an intellectual, an artist, a non-conformist. Books, art and politics were the tools.

6 April – *'Huw gave me 3 Albert Camus books cos we both like him.'*

12 April – *'Went over to the Campus West library. I got 4 books, Franz Kafka, Jean-Paul Sartre, and 2 George Orwell.'*

13 April – '*Read Orwell's* Keep the Aspidistra Flying. *It's a really brilliant book. Now I'm reading Sartre's* Nausea.'

19 April – '*Went to Welwyn. Bought a calculator and a couple of books – Jean-Paul Sartre and George Orwell.*'

4 June – '*Bought a couple of George Orwell books, and Sartre's* The Reprieve.'

It strikes me now that the books I was reading weren't necessarily the most helpful. They were gloomy and abstruse, and much of the time I was out of my depth. And there are so many obvious gaps. At school I was reading *Bleak House*, and *Emma*, *King Lear* and *Measure for Measure*, *The Collected Poetry of Robert Browning*; but when I got home, I would turn to these works, indulging my currently bleak outlook on life, using them to create an impressive persona more than anything else. Most obviously, I now notice the absence of any women writers on my list. I hadn't read *To Kill a Mockingbird* or *The Diary of Anne Frank*. I hadn't read *Little Women* or *The Bell Jar*. I hadn't read *Jane Eyre* or *Rebecca*. Equally, I wasn't reading Judy Blume, or Jackie Collins. I hadn't yet discovered feminism and so I read Sartre, but, shamefully, not de Beauvoir. Given some of the struggles I was having, I could come up with a reading list now that would have been a lot more help to me. Still, on I went, engaged in the pursuit of art and revolution.

13 June – *'Bought a kettle to use for my art exam. Had to batter it up though. Smashed it about with a brick and left it outside in the rain.'*

30 June – *'Went to party in Hatfield. All the young Conservatives standing around and sipping Pomagne. I got absolutely smashed and started insulting everyone.'*

I really did think I was quite the thing now, the height of sophistication.

30 March – At a party, *'Wore straight skirt, shirt, belt and stilettos. Had a Long Cool Screw!! Southern Comfort, gin and orange. LOVELY.'* It aged me overnight, as the next day at a pub I met boys I didn't like, and wrote, *'God they're so immature, they really bore me.'* Of course they did, with my mature and varied drinking tastes: *'I had a glass of wine before we went, then three Cinzanos and two Long Cool Screws. God I was absolutely pissed.'*

Debbie had left school and started work, where she met new people and went out to different places. In July I wrote: *'They went to loads of places up in London, very posh eh?'* London was exciting to me, and yet also threatening ('posh'), and I knew nothing about it, so would make errors that would mark me out as a true suburbanite: *'Deb went up to town. They went to Dean Street to a place called Pizzaland Express or something.'*

But in my ignorance, I didn't notice my errors, and

continued to believe that I had risen above those around me.

9 June – *'Went to Village Day after work. The part time punks were down there all tarted up in their latest trendy gear, bondage and berets. They amuse me cos they're so out of date.'*

Although some days it was as if I simply couldn't make up my mind about myself.

15 April – *'Easter holds none of the excitement it used to for me. I must be getting old and cynical. Only 16 and no fun any more.'*

16 April – *'Deb and I went to see* Superman. *It was really brilliant (perhaps I'm not so old and cynical after all).'*

Some of my fury was politically motivated and directed. Election fever was building up, and Mum had volunteered to help out the local Conservative Association, much to my dismay. There were party political broadcasts every night on telly, and the far right were very present and very scary, as they had been for some time.

18 April – *'Saw a Liberal election broadcast. That's all we hear now 24 hours a day – election election election. Saw the National Front on TV too. God they're so EVIL, they really are.'*

19 May – At a party, *'I ended up having intense political discussions with D for an hour. I was rather pissed and so I got a bit irate with all these prats who are a right bunch of Nazis. Music*

was chronic. Party was ok-ish.' And of course I wasn't just angry with strangers at parties, I was angry with my parents.

Debbie and I had recently decided we were Labour supporters, an act of rebellion as much as anything, which had more to do with buying punk records and straightening our jeans than actual politics. Labour vs Tory felt to me like a natural extension of Punks vs Squares. A girl at school wore a Vote Labour badge on election day and was told to take it off. (Imagine being told off for knowing there was an election happening. Nowadays you'd be made head girl.) When my daughters voted for the first time, in the London mayoral election of 2016, we were all in complete agreement about our politics. I'd been on at them to register as soon as they turned eighteen, then chased up their registration to get polling cards, then nagged them on the day to make sure they'd go. No cynical teenage ignoring of an election in this house. I may even have said, 'People died so you could vote.' You get the picture.

But come the day, both were quite excited – off they went to school, and then followed an afternoon of texts.

'Where's the polling station?'

'At the primary school.'

'But I can see a sign to another one?'

'Yes there are several.'

'I've forgotten my polling card!'

'You don't need it.'

'Do you do a tick or an X?'

'An X.'

'So I should take my ID right?'

'No you don't need any ID. Just tell them your name and address.'

'Hang on, I need my ID to buy a drink but not to vote? But I could be anyone.'

'Um, yes.'

'Should I take a pen?'

'No, there's a little pencil on a string.'

'Wait, what? I vote in PENCIL?'

'Um, yes.'

They'd got me worried by now. It did all seem a bit laid-back, a bit village hall. But by the time they got home, they felt empowered and adult, not least because they'd hit the target with their first shot. As the news came through that Sadiq Khan had won, and won decisively, they took it in their stride, taking for granted that your vote counts and that you have power.

Back in 1979, I'd had the opposite experience. I stayed up till 1.30 a.m. watching the results trickle in, and wrote in my diary next day, '*Most people at school were depressed. So – our first woman PM (pity it had to be Milk-Snatcher).*' That gloom was to stay with me through several more elections, as was the sense of political distance between me and my parents. It was not easy to discuss politics with them, Dad especially, and so it became something of a no-go area. The day before the election I'd written, '*Debbie has decided to vote Labour tomorrow and that really annoyed Dad. He gave one of his sermons and really went on and on being snide, patronising, v TORY. Annoyed me intensely – I just sat there fuming. Saw Coronation St and did some art.*'

I realise looking back that Dad had barely appeared in my diaries before this moment. I never thought to mention him while things were ok. A quiet, homely family man, we had got on well when I was a child, and he had taken us swimming, or to walk the dog in the woods. He didn't talk much, but I didn't mind when I was young, as it meant I could do all the talking. He had always been gentle and supportive, good humoured and calm, although something of a background figure, particularly to me. But he didn't react well to me and my sister growing into our teens, and becoming opinionated, assertive and challenging. He had no experience of – and therefore no way of dealing with – modern young women, and so his response to us was simply old-fashioned and unnecessarily confrontational.

This was partly just a result of the generation gap being wider then than it is now, but also, I can see in retrospect, down to his personal circumstances. He'd lost his beloved mother as a child, and then been brought up by a cold and distant stepmother, so I imagine he learned very early on to hide his feelings. Later, he would live through the London Blitz and then train as an RAF navigator. Those who survived the war, being offered no help or counselling afterwards, were a traumatised generation, burying their own wounds and then being irritated by youngsters who must have seemed to them to be spoilt and self-centred. My outbursts were the loud and direct opposite of all the lessons he'd learned about self-denial and self-repression, and must have felt like a rejection of his values.

And so, confronted with this difficulty, and unsure how to resolve it, his tactic was to dominate the conversation and try to shut us down. Arguments were not meant to be savoured, they were meant to be WON and ENDED. Perhaps because he didn't talk much, he couldn't quite see the point, and didn't enjoy the concept of debate. Silence was the aim. Talking about ideas, or accepting differing points of view, was to be avoided at all costs. Politics was a minefield, and although we tiptoed through it, explosions were common, causing injuries on both sides.

2017

Just before Christmas I booked a short holiday in Tenerife with my sister and her husband, our only worry being whether or not Dad would be ok while we were away. He'd had a couple of trips in and out of hospital, and ended up in a care home – frail, muddled, obviously declining. Much of his confusion had a kind of logic to it, rooted in denial of where he was. So he mistook the care home for the flat he used to live in, believing that my sister, who lived in the flat above, must have just popped downstairs each time she came to visit. Or he thought he was in a hotel and the carers were all staff; he would speak of popping down to reception, and of needing to pay his bills. This happened in hospital too. When he was leaving after his first stay of two weeks he became agitated about the cost, and we had to remind him of the existence of the NHS. It might have been partly that he remembered life before it, but was also a rejection of the idea that he was in hospital at all. He had strange, vivid hallucinations at night, when his oxygen levels dropped, telling me several times that all the beds were wheeled out of the ward each night and down to a huge underground room, possibly so they could clean the ward, he thought. Another time he told me that he had got a cab into town and spent the night on the top floor of the department store, Camp Hopson, where they had, quite unexpectedly, a kind of overnight drop-in shelter.

He never said any of the things you'd think someone in his situation might say. He never said, 'Oh God I miss Mum,' though he did more than anything. He never said, 'I just want to die,' as I know many old people do, and that was a relief. He did say, 'When am I coming home?' and 'When can we go out for dinner somewhere?', though he wouldn't have been able to cope with either of those things, being too weak, too deaf, too short of breath. Too bloody old, damn it.

One day we borrowed a wheelchair and wheeled him round the garden, but it was icy November, and even in a thick coat and hat and gloves he shrank down in the chair and was soon too cold. We looked at the glowing white silver birches and remarked how nice the bird feeders would be in spring, and then retreated back to the warmth of indoors.

I sat with Debbie while he played Scrabble with three other residents, one of them helped by a carer. The speed with which they chose their words astonished us. No need for an egg timer here to hurry things along, they slammed the letters down and moved the game on, pushing it forwards, impatient even while they were playing it. If it was only to pass the time, I got the feeling that they'd have liked it to pass quicker. I thought of those lines from *Waiting for Godot*.

> Vladimir: That passed the time.
>
> Estragon: It would have passed in any case.
>
> Vladimir: Yes, but not so rapidly.

When he died, it was the middle of the night. I got the call at 3 a.m., halfway through a bout of food poisoning. I'd vomited, and then lain groaning on the bathroom floor, clammy and grey faced, before staggering back to bed, where I lay shivering. My mobile rang and seeing it was my sister I knew at once what had happened.

Next day Debbie went to empty his room at the care home, which meant collecting the brand new, unworn, soft fluffy blue bathrobe I had bought him for Christmas, and which he had apparently regarded with utter disdain. She gathered up his other clothes, and a few ornaments and pictures, and looked for his mobile phone, before remembering that he'd thrown it in the bin a month or so earlier. 'It stopped working, bloody thing.' We assume he simply hadn't recharged it. 'Bloody phones,' he had said.

We'd cleared his flat out a few months earlier, when he moved into the care home. On that day, Debbie, Keith and I found ourselves standing in his empty flat, which already felt cold and deserted, faced with the task of dismantling his life. In the hallway the smoke detector, impossible to silence, emitted a shrill beep every ten seconds, as we set to work going through boxes and drawers and cupboards, sorting his belongings into separate piles – Keep, Donate, Throw Away. To add to the fun, it was Remembrance Sunday.

We found things which made us roll our eyes and laugh

– an enormous box marked FRAGILE proved to be full of nothing but packing straw, and though we picked through it carefully, half expecting to find a tortoise at the bottom, it was empty and mysterious. Other finds made us catch our breath – a sixtieth wedding anniversary card to Dad from our late mother, and in a small box, her engagement ring. The photo albums were piled up on the top wardrobe shelf, and for an hour we were distracted, drawn into this concertinaed version of our family history suddenly laid out before us. The earliest pictures showed our parents after the war but before the children. The wedding looked a bit demob austere but later, on Bournemouth beach, Mum was as slim and glamorous as Wallis Simpson, elegant in a summer dress, earrings and necklace, while Dad looked sporty in tennis whites. Still at the beach, our grandfather was in a full three-piece suit, resembling Jimmy Cagney.

Then came the '50s, and my brother was a toddler posing with a telephone, then my sister Debbie and I appeared, two years apart in age, and often dressed identically. There we were in our highly flammable nylon dressing gowns, in our side-by-side single beds. I could almost smell the Karvol on those rosebud printed pillowcases. Yes, Rosebud. I know. Everyone looked their best in the '60s, but that decade of chic was followed by '70s flounce – too much hair and trouser and collar, too many smocks and ponchos. And in the '80s photos we all looked older and frumpier than we do now – pie-crust collars, perms, pearls. Before you know it, our own children appeared, carbon copies of ourselves a few pages earlier.

Then, after the sweet diversion of all this reminiscing,

we found a tiny suitcase tucked in the bottom of the wardrobe. I clicked it open, and took out a thickly stuffed envelope, musty and fragile. Inside was Dad's RAF log book, and the complete record of his entry into the Air Force and training. A passport-sized photo showed him aged eighteen. My daughters were eighteen at the time, and safely studying science and art. He was studying navigation and bombing. I grew up knowing that Dad never fought in the war, because it ended just in time. But looking at the date on these papers, 1944, I realised that of course he was training while the war was still in full flow, in the clear expectation that he would be fighting. And knowing what that meant, in terms of survival rates for young pilots and navigators.

He never showed any of this to us; indeed, never made much of having been in the Air Force, never understood those who wanted to keep remembering. I don't think he was particularly proud of it; he'd simply had no choice. Had he been frightened? He never said. But still, he kept all these documents.

In the kitchen we went through the cupboards, which told a more recent history. The fridge spoke of neglect – sell-by dates ignored in a manner so cavalier as to be life-threatening. A freezer full of recently ordered ready meals he hadn't had time to eat. A tin of pease pudding that expired seven years ago. Flour we didn't dare open. In a cupboard was the caster sugar, still kept in the same shaker we used as children to dust pancakes, and in the drawer, a tiny paring knife we all remembered using to cut apples. Fifty years ago.

It was a sad thing to have to be doing but was made easier by doing it together. Afterwards, we all went to visit Dad. In the sitting room of the home was a large poppy display, and we asked him if there'd been any kind of Remembrance Day commemoration that morning. He said not, but then again, he might have just not remembered. Or not wanted to.

Debbie had visited him on the afternoon before he died. He was poorly, and in his bed; uncomfortable, and showing signs of a possible returning infection. But he said in a serious tone, 'Sit down, I want to say something.' 'What's this?' she wondered anxiously. 'I need to book a summer holiday. If I don't do it soon it'll be too late. I'm thinking a cruise. They can look after me, three meals a day, I won't have to walk far. Bring me in some brochures. Even if I don't go, they'll be something to look at.' When she told me, we laughed, at his irrepressible spirit, his defiance, his enduring love of a holiday. And I thought, this is life isn't it: imagining a future, planning, dreaming, choosing?

And so, after he'd died, and with the shock and the funeral out of the way, we decided we had to come on this planned trip to the Canary Islands, it's literally what he would have wanted, and yet it is not the holiday we expected, being infused not with worry, but with a strange mix of relief and regret, not least because the last time we were in this place, Dad was here too.

That was about five years before. He had been on good form, having rallied better than any of us had expected after Mum's death, and he had rented a mobility scooter, on which he'd bomb up and down the prom, stopping off at cafés along the way to have a Spanish brandy. He enjoyed doing nothing much at all on holiday. Eating, drinking, 'watching the world go by', as he used to say, and as I walk along the prom now with my sister, I realise that, as in most seaside places, there is lots of world-going-by to watch here.

The narrow flat stretch between the barren hills and the sea, into which the hotels and apartments are crammed, has nothing picturesque or classy about it, but a resolute cheerfulness pervades – the simple enjoyment of the sun, of daytime booze, of no work to go to. The holiday makers are either professional sunbathers with skin like a tan leather sofa, or those whose legs have never seen the light of day and are, as my youngest used to say, 'as white as a sheep'.

There are lots of walkers, like me and my sister, and lots of users of mobility scooters and wheelchairs who've found, like Dad, that the flat surface is ideal. I'd been more or less the youngest person on the plane out here, and over the tannoy the steward announced the safety info in a slow and sing-song voice, as if she was addressing a meeting of the Memory Club at the Eventide Rest Home. At the hotel there's a section of the breakfast buffet which Debbie calls 'Menopause Corner' – bee pollen, soy milk, almond milk, chia seeds, linseeds and beer yeast. Food for the hormonal older lady. But a room upgrade at the hotel gains you access to the brand new rooftop pool and sundeck, with a bar where all day long the drinks are free. Club Tropicana, in other words. I'm not sure they've reckoned on how much Brits on holiday will drink at a bar where all day long the drinks are free.

Along the prom the older holiday makers, of whom there are plenty, are interspersed with local hippies – a bunch of dreadlocked white boys with acoustic guitars, one singing a supper club version of 'I've Got You Under My Skin', and another sprawled in a shopping trolley with his fully plastered broken leg resting on the handles. A singing busker sets up every day in the underpass where the reverb flatters his voice. Further along, a row of empty café premises have been taken over by squatters – Kasa del Pirata is sprayed on one window, and a few lanky young men kick a football half-heartedly.

The area is touristy, and the sandwich boards outside the cafés advertise paella, fajitas and mojitos, and 'lasagne of the house', but then you round a headland and hit upon a stretch of black rocky beach and a sea full of surfers, and the scent of salty air replaces the smell of salty chips. I remember that when we were here with Dad, he decided that he wanted to buy a pair of shoes, the same as the ones he was wearing, which he'd bought here a few years before. And so we had set off into the streets back from the beach, the only thing approaching an 'old town', and searched for the exact lightweight, beige or grey leather shoes he liked to wear. Which apparently could only be found in Tenerife.

This single-mindedness was pretty typical. The other memory that now comes to me is that during that same trip I'd had a full-scale teenage blazing row with him one night over after-dinner drinks – something to do with the

NHS? Or the miners' strike? – which resulted in me storming up to my bedroom, shouting 'Good NIGHT' over my shoulder as I went. I was almost fifty years old at the time, and he could still make me feel sixteen and infuriate me like no one else.

But the immediate aftermath of his death had been all bureaucracy. Debbie had to speak to the GP, who had to speak to the coroner, who had to speak to the registrar. Then, as executors of his will, all three of us gathered at the solicitor's, with anti money-laundering proof of identity and residence, after a morning spent searching for something with my address on. The meeting with the funeral director took two hours and involved endless questions. Burial or cremation? Did we want him wearing anything in particular? Was anyone coming to view him at the undertaker's? Did he have a pacemaker? YES. It had to be removed before cremation, by a specialist. What kind of ceremony? What kind of coffin? What kind of flowers? How many cars?

We were calm and collected. Dad was ninety-one, his death not unexpected. How do you answer these questions when you are dazed with grief? We looked at the catalogue and flicked quickly past the pages of child-sized coffins. How on earth do you cope with that?

Humanist funerals are lovely, but pose more of a problem in terms of readings – without prayers and hymns you have to write proper eulogies, and find poems, so I spend an evening hunting through books, but everything seems too melodramatically sad, or too declamatory, or too mawkish, or trying too hard to be funny. Choosing the music is easier – Glenn Miller's 'Moonlight Serenade' as we walk in, and then Nat King Cole singing 'Stardust', which was Dad's favourite song. He had an irreplaceable old 78 record, which he got down from the loft once to play to my brother, who promptly knelt on it and cracked it clean in two. Ella Fitzgerald will sing 'Lullaby of Birdland' to buoy us up on our way out.

And it's the songs that make us weep, as ever. I'm set off as soon as I walk in, listening to Glen Miller, thinking of the war. Everyone else is gone during 'Stardust'. 'But that's what music is for,' I say to someone later, who seems to worry that we all cried too much. We weep with relatives we haven't seen for years, who know things about us no one else does, and yet who hardly know us at all in our current everyday incarnation. And funerals are where we construct a narrative of someone's life. The memories we recollect, or choose to recollect, are subjective and selective. They are the fragments we shore up against our ruin. We try to make some sense of it, and we leave out the bad bits, or at least the difficult bits.

Later, at home, I pour a massive gin and tonic and think how nothing would have made him happier. He did, oh how euphemistic, like a drink. When we cleared out his flat, we found in one cupboard INDUSTRIAL quantities of tonic – bought on special offer? Nuclear bunker-style quantities. The gin, obviously, bought on a weekly basis. A rack full of Spanish red wine. And Scotch, here there and everywhere.

I am reading Keggie Carew's *Dadland*, in which she recounts the story of her father's wartime exploits as a member of the Special Operations Executive forces, set against the backdrop of his declining memory. It's a fantastic book – hilarious, gripping, full of incident – and her larger-than-life father drives the narrative along, but it can't help but remind me of Dad. He was not such a spectacular character, nor did he have as spectacular a war – but something about that generation was unstoppable, uncomplaining, eternally bright-side looking. She speaks of her elderly father, muddled by dementia, saying of someone fifty years his junior, 'He's a bit younger than me, I think,' and she reasons it out thus: 'Dad has always seen himself as the brightest and freshest, and consequently, I suppose, by some curious deduction, the youngest in the room.' And that reminds me of our dad, complaining in the care home where he lived out his last few months that it was full of 'old people', defiantly making plans for lunches he wasn't well enough to attend, drinks he wasn't supposed to be drinking, and asking, the day before he died, for the cruise brochures.

On the front page of his funeral order of service we printed a photo of him in his RAF uniform, aged nineteen, the way he looked the day my mum met him. They'd been introduced as penpals via an uncle – my mum and her friend had written to this lonely young man, who was training in Jordan, and had each sent a photo. He chose Mum, and kept that very photo in his wallet for the rest of his life. They had exchanged letters and, when he was back in the UK, arranged to meet. He arrived, in his RAF blues, gliding up the escalator at Holborn tube, where she waited at the top. And I think of Powell and Pressburger's

A Matter of Life and Death. David Niven in that uniform, and the staircase to heaven. Wartime romance. Does anything tug the heart more strongly?

Back at home after the funeral, I put that photo of him up on Twitter. It's the most popular thing I've ever tweeted. He'd have been proud. Well, he'd have said, 'What the hell's Twitter?' and rolled his eyes, and we would have had a row about it. But still.

1979

After I'd finished my O-Levels, Dad took us all on a three-day trip to Paris. The company he worked for in London was French-owned and so he went there occasionally for work, little elements of French style creeping into his suburban Englishness: a love of cheese, red wine and Gauloises, which he smoked throughout my teens. Paris was thrilling to me, not surprisingly given all the Camus and Sartre I'd been reading, and one evening *'We went up to Montmartre, ate outside. Watched all the artists at work. They're brilliant. Lovely atmosphere there, students, musicians etc.'* A dream of how life could be.

Back at home I had moaned my way through my O-Levels.

28 June – The day they ended, *'Deb and I went up to London. Bought a Hawaiian shirt in the King's Road. Also some records – Toots and the Maytals, Echo and the Bunnymen, Evelyn Champagne King.'* Then came an induction into the VI form at school, which – inevitably – was boring.

2 July – '*First day as a VI former WOW tres dull. Got lectured all day about not wearing frayed jeans etc blah blah. Mum and Dad bought me some gorgeous trousers – pink with zips at the bottom.*'

But something was stirring in me, some inkling of how to escape this rut. It suddenly occurred to me that the only way out was to create something, to MAKE something happen. Up till now I had been waiting for it to land in my lap, been waiting for a boy to make my life start, shake things up, satisfy and fulfil me. The turning point, on which it all hinged, was buying a guitar.

3 August – '*I've decided to buy a guitar so I've been searching through all the* Melody Maker *ads and I think I've found one I want in Hackney.*'

It had to come from London. An urban guitar, dragging the city into my bedroom. I'm sure I could have found one at the music shop in Potters Bar. Or the record shop in Hatfield. A small ad in the back of the local paper. But this was about trying to become less suburban, to escape from who and where I was.

7 August – '*Met A at Potters Bar and we went up to Liverpool St. Got a train to London Fields and then managed to find this bloke's house. The guitar was really lovely – a black Les Paul copy. I bought it for £60 complete with hard case. Good bargain. Then we came home again. I played it nearly all evening – I'm really in love with it.*'

A good bargain. I knew nothing. I would have bought it even if it were broken.

It changed everything though, for better and worse. Already fed up with school, I became increasingly distracted. My O-Level results were about to come in, yet far from being stressed and anxious I was miles away, in a way that was considered quite normal at the time. A few years ago, when my daughters sat their GCSEs, they knew the exact moment of the exact day when their results would be available online, and sat in front of their screens from 8 a.m., clicking and clicking, loading and re-loading, until the email finally pinged into their inbox, which was followed by several hours of texting all their friends. They are a different generation, somehow they've been programmed to care about results. And my youngest, revising for his GCSEs as I write this, asked me one day, 'What did you get for your O-Levels, Mum?' and I had to tell him that I did well, but I couldn't remember exactly. 'My diary for 1979's right here though,' I said. 'I can have a look and find the day when I got my results.' So I flicked through, July, August, 'Ah, here we are. Thursday, August the 23rd. Right, what does it say?' I read it quickly to myself, and then edited it for his ears. For it was even more distracted than I could have imagined.

23 August – *'Got my O-level results. I passed them all. Debbie phoned, she's going out with P tomorrow. Phoned G – he's probably going to the Civic on Sat. Huw phoned – he's trying to get on the guest list on Sat. C's parents came home, found out people had been*

round and hit the roof! They even searched the dustbin for cigarette ends!! Then they found one of D's roll ups and accused us of smoking pot!! They caused a real scene. Can't wait to go home.' I had been staying with a friend while her parents were away, and indeed, although I sound outraged at the accusation, we had had a party, despite being forbidden to do so. A gang of boys had stayed the night, there was booze and cigarettes and sex, and yes, probably pot, even though I was so affronted by her parents' suspicions. The parent in me is now entirely on their side. And I still can't quite remember what my O-Level results were. I hadn't thought to write them down. Too boring.

The guitar was my best friend now, and I was energised by it. Pretty soon I would start to write songs, and some of what was going into the diaries would go into lyrics. I didn't quite know it yet, but this would be an escape route, a catalyst for all that followed. But for now, the guitar simply added a new dimension to my moping.

7 September – *'Didn't do much at school today. Had English and Economics. Heard The Jam on the radio. Came home, played guitar, talked to Debbie, played records, went for walk, had bath, washed hair. Routine. Dull. But I don't care cos I'm in love and I'm still only 16 (not for long).*

My sister had started at Pitman's secretarial college, and I too had started typing lessons at school. Mum had been a secretary, and this was the most normal and obvious career path for a girl. Nothing in me thought this was unusual or rebelled against the implied expectations. It was talked about as 'something to fall back on'.

Instead, I rebelled against the passing of time, and life in general.

25 September – '*Watched Rickie Lee Jones on OGWT* [Old Grey Whistle Test]. *She was great. God, I'm 17 tomorrow. Wish I could be 16 forever. I'm not going to school though. Me and Deb are gonna go up to London shopping.*'

26 September – '*Not 16 any more / sad birthday.*'

A week later I joined a band, and carried on hating school.

5 November – '*I've got an economics test tomorrow and I'm just not doing any work at school. All I wanna do is play guitar all the time and write songs. Oh I hate being at school. Now I feel really miserable.*'

12 November –'*Don't think I'll come to school tomorrow cos I've got to give in a history essay that I haven't done and I've got an English test – can't face it.*'

13 November – '*Didn't go to school today. Got up about 12. Had a bath. Taped the Specials LP. Watched* The Love Boat. *Mum had another go at me about my clothes / my hair / the band / The Boyfriend and his skinhead haircut (haha) / etc etc BORING. Watched* Not the Nine O'Clock News. *It was really funny.*'

The parent rows had started in earnest. Some were provoked by my boyfriend's appearance more than anything – he looked like a punk, with a very short, suedehead haircut.

15 December – '*Mum in foul mood – nasty about The Boyfriend – said I can't go to rehearsal tomorrow. He came round about 8 and she didn't speak to him.*'

16 December – '*Mum was really obnoxious all day. I was miserable cos I couldn't go over to The Boyfriend's. God, she's such an old bat. I really hate her sometimes.*'

18 December – '*Got home from school – Mum said she wanted to talk to me and she broke down and cried all over me, apologising and saying that she'd made a mistake etc. She's realised she was stupid to judge The Boyfriend by the length of his hair and I can see him whenever I want to. I was amazed.*'

My mum and I were standing on opposite sides of a canyon now, shouting at each other, not hearing, not understanding. I'd behaved worse than this in the past, and they hadn't objected, so was this conflict linked to my growing creative life? Did they sense something in me breaking away, turning my back on them? Youth culture, tribalism, music, creativity, all of this was a kind of modern, urban misbehaviour, and more alarming to them than pubs, snogging older boys, or cars on country lanes. I told them I wanted to marry a poet and live in London. I wanted to get out. I couldn't understand why they had ever moved here in the first place. Why would anyone want to? Who would choose suburbia?

It was intended to be utopian. Although when twentieth-century critic Ian Douglas Nairn coined the term 'subtopia', he was very much sneering at everything he felt had gone wrong with England's architecture and design, suburban style having, in his opinion, encroached upon and ruined the landscape. Yoking together the words suburban and utopia, you end up with a description of something that is clearly sub-standard. Very much less than utopian. A suburban dystopia.

But then, even the word 'suburb' itself has a kind of negative connotation, coming from the Latin *suburbium*, which is a joining together of the words *sub* (under) and *urbs* (city). We use it to mean, more or less, the outskirts of the city, or the residential areas that surround a city, being within easy reach of the urban workplace. And yet we must sense within the word itself the implication that the suburb is ranked below the city, is inferior in some way. Or even that it is literally below the city, located underneath it – subterranean, hidden. Like a crypt. Is it where all the bodies are buried? It's certainly where all the secrets are hidden.

American cinema often uses suburbia as the dystopian location for shocking or deviant behaviour. David Lynch, for instance, specialises in that queasy juxtaposition of the apparently idyllic with its exact opposite. The opening of *Blue Velvet* is dazzling – a too-white picket fence, a blindingly vivid blue sky, roses the colour of arterial blood, the husband happily watering the lawn, smiling children safely crossing the road. But within minutes the scene descends into nightmare after a freakish accident, and then the camera pans down through the grass, into the soil below, where insects writhe in the mud. 'Look what's REALLY going on,' it seems to say. 'All this is here, all the time, you just won't see it.' The suburban dream suddenly seems creepy, as if its relentless NICEness is only pretend, and can't survive without repressive conformity and wilful blindness.

Brookmans Park was the epitome of that type of suburban aspiration and idealism. An exclusive enclave, it was posher than nearby Welham Green and Hatfield, which were more mixed and had council houses, many of them lived in by my school friends. But there was a divide between the two sections of the village, an actual hill to be climbed, and an aspirational one. We lived at the bottom of that hill, and the house I grew up in was by no means luxurious. Two-and-a-half beds upstairs plus bathroom, kitchen, lounge and dining room downstairs, it housed the five of us. My sister and I shared a bedroom, while Keith had a tiny boxroom, and Mum and Dad the larger bedroom at the front. There was no central heating, and we would take a paraffin heater into the bathroom if having a bath, snuggling up with hot water bottles at night.

When I was five or six we had an extension built, which added two more bedrooms, bringing us more into line with Brookmans Park's high standards. At the same time we 'knocked through' downstairs, and got a downstairs loo and a shower, and a bigger kitchen, all of which meant we ended up with a comfortable amount of space for a family of five. I moved into the new small bedroom. The other small bedroom became a 'study', which meant it housed a collection of encyclopaedias, and Dad's wine-making equipment.

But there was no getting away from it – we were in a semi-detached house, which we had stretched as far as it would go, and Mum never overcame her jealousy of anyone in a detached. It was her great goal in life. Why did she so set her heart on this? I think it was the place itself that did it to her, the proximity of houses that were sold as dream homes. And she didn't invent the dream, it was invented for her, and marketed to her. It was implicit in the very design and concept of the suburban garden village, and there from the moment when economic depression of the 1930s made the houses harder to sell, forcing the developers to advertise. Seductive brochures were created, describing all the attractions of the location and the houses.

'Brookmans Park, a real country home within 35 minutes of Town,' one such read. 'The opportunity of living in a house with all modern conveniences, on one of the great ancestral estates of England, absolutely unchanged and undisturbed in its essential character, that is what Brookmans Park offers you. The plan of the estate is absolutely to avoid crowding any portion of it with brickwork. Every house will be built well back from the roadway, giving dignity and seclusion, and leaving the original spaciousness of the avenues unspoilt. You will be able – not merely this year but always – to glance out of your windows at some of the loveliest scenery in England, at hills and valleys, rugged old trees and wide meadows. A few minutes walk will take you to one of the three delightful lakes, to Gobions Wood, the Italian sunken garden with its lavender and water lilies surrounded with lawns and giant cedars.'

The brochures drew attention to the excellent transport links, especially the trains during the 'rush hours'. 'The latest Theatre Train leaves King's Cross at 12.15 a.m.' Prices were reasonable, a three-month season ticket to Kings Cross costing £4 8s. And 'a fleet of single decker pneumatic tyred buses run through the estate'.

A building company called Phillips Brothers issued their own brochure: 'Houses erected on the Brookmans Park Estate are attractive and arresting. To the wife because their appearance is pleasing and they are planned to save as much time and trouble as possible; to the husband because the call on his pocket is so reasonable for houses of this type . . . The Kitchen, a joy to the housewife, is tiled . . .'

My mum was this housewife. The whole thing might as well have had her name on it. She'd grown up in Kentish Town and Dad in Finsbury Park, and both had been bombed, and of course anyone who'd been through that might want to get out of London, and might think the suburbs looked like heaven. If the brochure seemed idyllic in the 1930s, how much more so after the war? My parents moved first to a flat in Barnet, and then in 1956 bought our 1930s house in Brookmans Park. The road was still unfinished and full of potholes, into which they would empty the ashes from the coal fire.

It was all about escape. How could I not see that? Everyone wanted to leave; everyone wanted something better. Mum's parents moved to Radlett, and then to the sea at Broadstairs. Two of her brothers moved out to Surrey (gallingly, into detached houses in proper stockbroker-belt territory). The other brother emigrated to Canada. As for my dad's brother, he too moved to Brookmans Park, first living in the same road as us, and on the 'wrong' side, which backed onto the railway line, before – oh woe! – moving up to a detached house in Moffatts Lane. Leaving us as the only family members stuck in a little semi, which was NOT so little, of course, but the symbolism was strong.

This was one of the anxieties about suburbia in the '60s and '70s – a fear that the urban working class had been broken up and thus disempowered by moving out of the city. The term used to describe the subsequent attempt to become more middle class was 'embourgeoisement', which really just means social climbing, though it contains within it a strong sense of disapproval. Left-wing social commentators thought that it was dangerous for working people to lose their solidarity and sense of unity as a class, realising that once they were broken up into self-contained, individualistic, semi-detached home owners, they would be likely to vote Conservative. And this was clearly true, Mum and Dad being textbook examples.

In Hanif Kureishi's *The Buddha of Suburbia*, narrator

Karim says, 'the proletariat of the suburbs did have strong class feeling. It was virulent and hate-filled and directed entirely at the people beneath them.' I think of my parents, both originally from working-class families, each of their fathers starting out as train drivers, calling other people 'common'. And then the irony of the fact that they themselves, and people like them, ended up being looked down on by both sides: not properly of the middle class in that they were not educated or cultured, they could then also be sneered at from the left, for being too privatised in their thinking, too keen on improving their own personal lot, too keen on buying things. Nice things, even. Although, when I think about that, I always think of the quote from *Lucky Jim*: 'There was no end to the ways in which nice things are nicer than nasty ones.'

They had chosen green outdoor space instead of dirty old brick, clean fresh air instead of pea soup fog, newness instead of dereliction, fields instead of bomb sites. Inevitably, they saw the suburbs, even after the war had ended, as a place of greater safety, representing security along with comfort, and freedom from anxiety. Brookmans Park itself had experienced a good war, being far enough from London to mostly escape. A couple of bombs had fallen – possibly aimed at the BBC transmitting station; there were ambulances stationed at the golf club, and a warden's first aid post, and a local Home Guard, which was run by the village GP Dr Dwyer, who was still the GP when my parents first moved there. By the end of the war though, the village had come through unscathed, and still looked as good as new.

It's taken me many years, but I understand what drew them here. I now live in what is derisively called a metropolitan bubble, where all my friends share my liberal values and echo back at me my instinctive response to the world. Yet there's another level of instinct in me, perhaps deeper and buried, the voices of my parents and my childhood neighbours, which also informs my thinking. I don't always agree with those voices, any more than I did in my teens, but they provide a counterbalance, and still something to kick against. I like to think I'm London, but in fact, like many people, I have suburban bones.

1980

A W.H. Smith pocket diary with a black cover, one page per day. The usual tube map, bank holidays, metric conversion tables – and then lots of little folded-up pieces of paper tucked inside the opening pages, all bearing boys' phone numbers. Alan, Steve, Frank, Terry, Colin. I was seventeen years old. I had stopped mentioning what was on the telly. Instead, I read *Testament of Youth*, and watched *Rebel Without a Cause*, *Badlands*, *Klute*, *Dark Victory* (sharing a love of Bette Davis with my mum), *Annie Hall*, *Manhattan*, *Gaslight* and *The Misfits*.

I was in a relationship now, but I was a terrible girlfriend – and I'm really very sorry. I was self-obsessed, melo-dramatic, disloyal, inconsistent, unpredictable and argu-mentative. Conflicted, repressed, driven, shy, self-conscious, romantic, young and curious. I dreamed of being in love more than I actually was in love with anyone. I had no idea what I wanted and was obsessed by my own feelings while careless of those around me. *'This is all getting a bit deep,'* I wrote one day, when my boyfriend was unhappy. One day I'd like him, the next day not. *'Basically I just can't cope with going out with someone – I go on and off him about every 10 minutes.*

It's just so confusing.' I was desperate for and terrified of sex, having had the horror of its negative outcomes and implications drummed into me from such an early age. Fear of pregnancy meant that I didn't fully trust any form of contraception, and my awareness of parental disapproval was overwhelming.

Everything was conflict and secrecy, and both seemed part of the very fabric of suburbia. I recently found a notebook of mine, in which I had written quotes from books I liked. I'd copied out this from Margaret Drabble's *The Waterfall*: 'When I was at home, in my parents' home, I felt all the time afraid that any word of mine, any movement, my mere existence, might shatter them all into fragments. As a small child, not yet knowing why, I practised concealment, deviously reconstructing my every thought for them, knowing that if they could see me as I truly was they might never recover from the shock.'

Although, maybe it's inevitable that teenagers lie, wherever they live, however they're brought up. I said to someone recently, as my only piece of advice on the parenting of teenagers, 'Be prepared for them to lie to you.' I thought I had lied because I had to – because I didn't want to confront my parents, and because the rules were too strict. But I've been more liberal with my kids, and we've always been more open with each other. I said to them, 'I don't mind much what you do, just don't lie to me. I like to know where you are.' And one by one, at various times, for various reasons, they have all lied to me. Sometimes for good, or understandable reasons: to protect me, to stop me worrying about something they knew was ok. Sometimes just not to have to talk about something. In other words, it makes me think, teenagers NEED to lie. It doesn't mean that parenting has failed. It's part of the process of breaking away, and forging a separate identity. Having private information is their version of the blank page.

It's possible too, that the blank page in my diary I mentioned earlier sounds more dramatic than it actually is. For what had happened on that day was not an unspeakable crime, or a trauma that left me wordless, it was a fairly commonplace teenage experience, more mortifying than anything else. The blank page represents embarrassment and secrecy, an unwillingness to describe and also a desire to keep a secret from my mum.

But it's something else too, I now realise; it's about power and control, in the way that writing always is. I'm still not going to tell you what was on that page, and I am still the one deciding how much of myself I reveal. All this quoting from my diary looks confessional, looks exposing, but there are pages I'm not showing you. The blank page shows that process happening even while I was writing the diary. However subconsciously, I was shaping a narrative, choosing what to put in and what to leave out.

I was interviewed after writing *Bedsit Disco Queen* by a journalist who made the point that, for such an apparently private person, wasn't it surprising that I had made the decision to write a revealing and intimate book, giving away details about myself and my life that you might imagine I'd prefer to keep under wraps. It gave me pause for thought, especially as I was at that moment about to embark on writing a fortnightly column for the *New Statesman*, in which I was bound to draw on personal experiences, and tell stories about things that happened to me. In other words, invading my own privacy.

The answer I gave in the interview, though, was to say that writing about yourself is very different to being written about. When you write a memoir, or a column in a magazine, you are the one in control. The 'secrets' you give away are only those you are comfortable with, and many more remain hidden from view, just as they should. You may be shining a light on to your own life, but you are the one holding the lamp, and can angle it in whichever direction you choose. Even in your most honest moments, you will probably lean towards showing yourself in a good light, or as good as possible, opting for words that are at least, as Larkin put it, 'not untrue, and not unkind'.

This point was made brilliantly by Chris Heath in his recent book *Reveal*, about the life and career of Robbie Williams. Talking about the singer's propensity for self-exposure, for sharing more than most people do, Heath writes: 'Most people try to protect themselves by clutching their secrets close, but there is another way. If you reveal your secrets, share your stories, before anyone else can discover them, then they're so much harder to use against you.

And also, this way, even as you share them, they remain yours.'

I think that's very true – that controlling what you tell and when means that you retain ownership of the details of your life. Being interviewed, on the other hand, is an entirely different thing, and in many ways a much scarier prospect. I have many journalist friends, and it never fails to amaze them when I inform them that we – and by this I mean anyone who's ever been interviewed – are often afraid of them. We don't know what to expect when they turn up, whether they want us to be garrulous or mysterious, live up to our image or confound it, be starry or down to earth. Different interviewers want different things, and it's not always obvious until afterwards, when you read the piece they've written. And this is the source of the fear – a conversation takes place between two people in a room, but only one of them gets to tell what happened. One half of the encounter determines whether the other half is funny or dull, clever or stupid, nice or nasty. Paradoxically, reading an interview with yourself you can feel strangely silenced. You may recognise the words you said, but they may seem jumbled, or out of context, and most important, your impressions of what happened, or what the interviewer was like – whether they were funny or dull, clever or stupid, nice or nasty – go completely unrecorded, your version of events goes unheard. An interview is an apparently informal, relaxed chat, at the end of which YOU WILL BE JUDGED. In print.

Compared to that, when you write about yourself, you hold all the cards, and that's liberating. I look again at that blank page in the diary, and I'm quite proud of it, of what it represents. I understood, even then, that writing things down was risky, that words were powerful, that there was strength in the unsaid. Nothing – no memoir, no song – is ever completely confessional, and writing is always about knowing who's in charge.

And in my diary, I think it was a way of wresting back some power without having to be confrontational. Both my sister and I had boyfriends we were forbidden to see, who we saw in secret. I would sneak out of school, and spend afternoons in the park, and it was almost more exciting than just going out with him. But the grown-ups had a pact of solidarity, and my mum had a network of spies. Someone told her they'd seen me in town with my boyfriend.

15 January – '*One of Mum's darling golfing friends told her she saw me down town last week and mum accused me of playing truant. Old bat.*' Then someone else phoned to tell her about Debbie and her forbidden boyfriend. The lines were drawn so narrowly that it was easy to cross them, but hard to get away with. Our secrets and lies were undone by snoopers and spies.

28 January – '*Awful day. Mum had another go at me about The Boyfriend – how awful he is etc – virtually forbade me to see him. Decided I've had enough of it so I phoned him to suggest we give it a rest for a while.*'

Two days later, instead, '*We decided to see each other whenever we can in secret. How exciting! And so it goes on . . .*'

21 February – '*Had row with mum – same old things – she went out and I got v depressed. I've decided to chuck The Boyfriend. I*

like him but I'm getting a bit bored.' So I dumped him, made myself cry, and got back together with him three days later.

13 May – *'When I got home Mum confronted me with the fact that she knows I've been seeing The Boyfriend – but she doesn't seem to mind and she wants me to bring him home. God, I just do not understand her. I KNEW she'd find out sooner or later though.'*

I really didn't understand her at all, and how could I. We'd been so close, and were now so far apart, and we were so alike, and now so unalike, that it was agony for both of us. She'd invented my childhood, creating my memories with the stories she told me: of Keith's asthma attack, and the hamster biting the doctor, and Debbie sitting stoic and silent while Mum tweezered a large thorn out of her forehead. Me cheerfully rolling eggs across the kitchen floor like marbles, or adding salt to Debbie's glass of Disprin. I stored it all up, and then added some memories of my own, moments that hinted at a possible distance between us.

The Top 40 was broadcast on Radio One at lunchtime on Tuesdays, just after *Newsbeat*. A molly-coddled, fussy-eater of a child, I was allowed to walk home every day for lunch, and the great benefit of this – apart from getting to have oxtail soup and a cheese roll every day, safe from any encounter with school semolina – was that I heard the freshly revealed chart every week, and the new number one single, before anyone else. This was the early 1970s, and the charts were the usual perplexing mess of ill-assorted singles, none of them sitting comfortably next to each other or making much sense as a coherent whole; and even individual records could be mystifying to a ten-year-old. Pop music might have been derided for being drivel with inane lyrics, but to an inquisitive child like me, everything was potential new knowledge – What's a metal guru? What's a convoy? Don McLean's 'American Pie' threw new words at me in every verse – What's a chevy, Mum? What's a levy? – and for the first, though not the last time, caused me to feel actual embarrassment about a pop song. Those lyrics, about this being the day that he'll die, they were so serious, so heavy. They brought something looming and dark into the house and made us feel uncomfortable. And I was intrigued, and my ears pricked up, but not for the first or the last time, when encountering something dark and difficult, Mum tried to laugh it off – 'Well, THAT'S not a very cheerful song, is it?' before changing the subject. Something had been revealed to me about what people might write in songs, and what the response might be. We were so close, Mum and me, and then occasionally I'd get a glimpse of how far apart.

But then came my teenage years, and all the trouble and strife. I thought I was just furious with her and she was The Enemy, until one day, at university, I read *The Female Eunuch* and came across all sorts of sentences that clicked with me. The battles I'd had with femininity, the feeling that I wasn't cut out to be a conventional girl, which led me to the androgyny of punk – all of that had caused me problems at home. Mum would criticise both my appearance and my behaviour for being too aggressive, too contrary, too unfeminine. I had anguished over some of this, wondering if it was me that was at fault, and so when in 1982, twenty years old and taking a Women in Literature course at Hull University, I first read Germaine Greer, she spoke to me of things I'd long thought and felt without ever having words or names for. 'What we ought to see in the agonies of puberty is the result of the conditioning that maims the female personality in creating the feminine.'

In other words, it wasn't me that was wrong, I wasn't a 'failed girl' as I'd sometimes felt, it was the expectations that were wrong, and which had attempted to crush my natural spirit. The generation gap between me and my mother was made worse by the fact that her generation had almost entirely conformed to the conventions of the feminine ideal, and so, as Greer pointed out, they were then obliged to carry on this process, acting it out upon their daughters – 'We could see that our mothers black-mailed us with self-sacrifice, even if we did not know whether or not they might have been great opera stars or the toasts of the town if they had not borne us. In our intractable moments we pointed out that we had not asked to be born . . . We knew that they must have had motives of their own for what they did with us and to us. The notion of our parents' self-sacrifice filled us not with gratitude, but with confusion and guilt.'

This resonated with me, the way in which I was made to feel guilty for wanting something different from what Mum had wanted, and what she wanted for me. And so the book gave me a theoretical analysis and a language for instinctive feelings – my discomfort with gender stereotypes, the restrictions placed upon girls, and the low expectations that had set limits for me and my friends. Greer's descriptions of the role of the conventional wife-mother are bleak and doomy – 'mother is the dead heart of the family', she wrote – and it's salutary to remember how powerless women still were at the time she wrote it; the Equal Pay Act was not yet in force, women were unable to secure mortgages without the signature of a husband or father, and so on. And so she paints a brutal picture of utterly hopeless drudgery – 'The unfortunate wife-mother finds herself anti-social . . . The home is her province, and she is lonely there. She wants her family to spend time with her for her only significance is in relation to that almost fictitious group. She struggles to hold her children to her, imposing restrictions, waiting up for them, prying into their affairs. They withdraw more and more into non-communication and thinly veiled contempt.'

This was my life right here on the page! Only just out of my teens, this read to me like a manifesto of all that could go wrong and had gone wrong, and set me on a determined course not to follow in these footsteps. I could do this by living out my life in a different pattern, and that I fully intended to do; but there was another way in which I could act upon this new and eye-opening information – I could write about it. I had been in bands since my late teens, and was writing songs, so it hit me like a thunderbolt when I read this passage:

'The supreme irony must be when the bored housewife whiles away her duller tasks, half-consciously intoning the otherwise very forgettable words of some pulp love song.

159

How many of them stop to assess the real consequences of the fact that "all who love are blind" or just how much they have to blame that "something here inside" for? What songs do you sing, one wonders when your heart is no longer on fire and smoke no longer mercifully blinds you to the banal realities of your situation? (But of course there are no songs for that.)'

Well, why not? I thought. And if Germaine's right and there aren't any songs for that, then I'd better set about writing some. Up until that point my lyrics had been mostly about relationships, and while they may have taken a more realistic look at love than the old standards quoted by Greer, they nonetheless stayed mostly within this familiar territory. Now I began to write songs about the lives of girls and women, inspired by what I had read. The lyrics to 'Frost and Fire' put into words the feelings I'd had about the distance between mine and my mother's life ambitions – 'And when you claim you wouldn't change a day / It makes me wonder where I went astray / Happy with things that leave me tired / We're as unalike as frost and fire.' The song 'Bittersweet' was an attack on the femininity I'd had foisted upon me – 'She's such a sweet girl, free of the taints of this world / Think that's a compliment, don't be so full of sentiment / Why d'you worship sweetness? What virtue's there in weakness? / Being pushed about is nothing much to shout about I know.'

But then I re-read *The Female Eunuch* recently, wondering whether it would still resonate with me in the same way. And this time I was struck by passages in the book where Greer can be dismissive, proscriptive even, telling women

160

how they ought to behave, what they ought to want. I'm a mother now, so I wasn't quite so comfortable with the tone of some of the book. When I was young, I could sneeringly direct the put-downs towards the older generation, but now, when I read a sentence like this – 'Bringing up children is not a real occupation, because children come up just the same, brought or not' – or this – 'One of the deepest evils in our society is tyrannical nurturance' – I have to admit that it stings, and that it feels too close for comfort to plain old woman-blaming; that idea that whatever you do as a mother, it's bound to be wrong.

I had blamed my mother. I had thought that whatever she did it was bound to be wrong. I wrote that my mother and I were as unalike as frost and fire but almost the opposite was true. My ambitions and my education and my career, all those things drove us apart. Then years passed and I had kids, and for a while I stopped recording and touring – something that was only possible because of the career success I'd already achieved – and ironically, it brought me closer to my mother than we had been for years, perhaps since my childhood, although it still wasn't without effort. But stopping work for a while was a luxury, and it lasted only as long as it took me to start needing once again to make things, at which point I wrote a book, and started recording again.

Then came my menopause, and I went a bit mad. Along with the night sweats and sudden mood swings, the unaccountable rages and tears and irritability, came a worsening of the anxiety from which I'd always suffered, triggering days and nights of catastrophic thinking, terror, overwhelming and inescapable thoughts of doom and disaster, illness, imprisonment, death and loss. And I remembered what Mum had been like when I was a teenager, and the fact that she would have been menopausal, having had a hysterectomy after a cancer scare, which, of course was never described to us at the time as a cancer scare, but which must have been terrifying, and which triggered an abrupt and extreme menopause.

This is the diary entry I find hardest to read now, because of what it tells me about her.

5 April 1978 – '*Got up about 10.30. Deb had a driving lesson. Mum went to the doctor and got some tranquillisers to calm her down a bit! Watched* Crown Court.'

Look how little I cared, or understood. Well fair enough, I was only fifteen. But it hits me hard now. For she did try to talk about her complicated feelings. She did try to ask for help. She broke the code and admitted to feeling something, and she went to the doctor and she was put on Valium.

I think back now to those rows we had, her sudden anger and equally sudden tearful apologies. Classic mood swings, I now see. Her vigilance, even her snooping, which drove me to despair, was the result of fretting about me, much of it justified. I remember now how she used to fear the worst, and stories she told of waking up panicked in the middle of the night, tossing and turning with endless worry. And I would roll my eyes and laugh at her. We all did. It was a common response to anxiety, which wasn't even given that name at the time. Nowadays, it is a widely acknowledged mental health issue, and there have been books and articles galore about panic attacks, hypochondria and generalised anxiety. As someone who waited until my fifties to confront a condition that had plagued me for much of my adult life, I'm grateful that it is becoming easier and less shameful to talk about.

And it is shameful, that's part of its power. We're all getting better at acknowledging the seriousness of psychological issues, but anxiety has one big problem in this respect, which is that we see it as funny. Depression isn't funny, it's quite literally sad, and while not always easy to own up to, it does at least nowadays have the advantage of seeming real.

Anxiety on the other hand – and I should stress again that I speak here as a sufferer, and this is how we often talk about our problem – is just silly. It's worrying about nothing. It's making a fuss, being a bore. It's the opposite of cool. If the ultimate modern pose is the teenage lack of affect, then anxiety is its antithesis, and saddles you with the niggly, nagging behaviour of an over-protective mum, seeing danger everywhere, catastrophising, avoiding risk, clinging to safety like a piece of floating wreckage. It makes us do things that feel foolish even while we are doing them. Afterwards we try to laugh, to shake it off, reduce the size of its terrifying shadow and prove that we can see the joke too. I'm only just beginning to learn that while laughing is mostly a good thing, sometimes we also have to take ourselves seriously, and forgive the dumb things our brains make us do.

But that's so easy for me to say, because I didn't have to go through my menopausal meltdown in 1970s suburbia. Instead I was in talky middle-class north London, with money for therapy and massages, and an app on my phone for daily meditation and a group of women friends all going through the same thing, with whom I walked and talked, sharing our experiences and our fears, our nuttiness. Some of us tried HRT, but none of us got casually put on Valium as my mum did. Instead we went to our doctors, who told us about mindfulness.

Mum had always been clever but, in a family with three brothers and a Victorian father, there was no choice for her but to leave school at fifteen and work for a few years as a secretary. In later years, when I was living in a terraced house in north London, she would say to my sister, 'I don't know WHY Tracey lives there, honestly, she could buy a castle in Scotland for the price of that house!' A bizarre thing to say, knowing that I loved living in London, and even more bizarre when I think that, as a young woman, she had loved it too. Growing up, she had been sociable and outgoing; slim and pretty, she loved dancing, liked a drink and a smoke, wore too much pancake make-up, which rubbed off on Dad's collar when they were courting.

One night, while he was still in the RAF and before they were married, Dad came home unexpectedly on leave and, arriving at her house, was told by her mother that Mum had gone out dancing with someone else. Infuriated but determined, Dad turned up at the dance hall to confront her. The other man had just bought her a cherry brandy, so Dad insisted on buying her one too. I picture her there, with a cherry brandy in each hand, the two men glaring at each other, eyes locked in a duel, Mum feeling awkward and guilty but probably THOROUGHLY ENJOYING HERSELF. And I think, 'She was game, she was a laugh. I'd have been friends with her.'

Working as a secretary in Holborn, she and the other office girls would look out of the window at the working girls on the street below, trying to figure out what was the signal the girls gave to passing men which would cause them to turn on their heels and follow them. She'd walk back home to Kentish Town through thick pea-soup fogs, and was adept at surviving as a young, single woman on public transport. Once, a man sat too close, pressing against her in an intrusive way, and she said in a loud voice, 'Would you like to sit right ON my lap?'

This bold, London girl would have understood perfectly why I didn't want to live in a castle in Scotland. Somewhere along the line she just forgot. I had ended up living half a mile from where she'd grown up, yet it had become completely alien and incomprehensible to her, like another planet. After marrying and becoming a mother, Mum and Dad moved out of London and she stopped work, focusing all her energy and attention on raising us children, and she was good at it, really good at it, and happy for years and years. When I picture her, it is almost always at home. In the sitting room on a glaring summer's afternoon with the curtains tightly drawn watching Wimbledon on the TV. Or standing at the ironing board singing along with a Jack Jones record, much to the derision of Keith, who was the cool teenager in the house, and for whom she had bravely gone out one day to buy a 'Zed Leppelin' LP. Or sitting in her armchair after Christmas lunch, tapping open a Chocolate Orange, and hoping against hope that the TV movie wouldn't be a war film, but a proper women's film, preferably starring Bette Davis, or failing that, anything with Paul Newman in it. Or with Dad, doing that skilful dance that couples do around each other in the kitchen, knowing each other's part of the routine, as Sunday lunch was prepared – Mum producing dishes from the oven, and getting hot and flustered in the process, Dad in charge of music in the sitting room.

I was the last of those children, and so as I careered through my teens the empty nest was looming. Mum and I had been exceptionally close, bonded by years of togetherness and an essentially similar temperament, and so my teenage rebellion was especially hurtful to her, and came at a time when she had no resilience to cope with it and no language in which to talk calmly and openly about such complicated feelings. The code of secrecy, and the times, and the pressure of keeping up appearances, all worked against her, and against the pair of us.

When she died I was in my late forties, and yet she spent her last few weeks telling me off, which was the most reassuring aspect of that whole time. 'Are you still here?' she kept saying when she'd look up to see me at her hospital bedside. 'Don't cancel anything, get on with your life.' And more or less the last thing she said to me when I sat by her the day before she died, was 'Go on, don't hang around here, you'll miss your train. I'm watching that clock you know.'

Halfway through the next day, after several difficult hours, I was in the room as she took her last breath, and afterwards, as I sat there for a few minutes, all I could think of to say was, 'Thank you.' And then I wept for three days straight, crying till I couldn't see, crying in the kitchen, at the front door with a friend who brought flowers, and in the shower, where the tears streamed down my body and washed away, washed away.

2016

Standing still, in the centre of the village, I see that the Brookmans Park Hotel has now been rebranded as simply BROOKMANS. It's time for a break from my exploring, so I make my way over and inside find a very stylish bar/restaurant, where I order a cappuccino. Three mums are having coffee and talking about books, films and plays – *Harry Potter, The Curious Incident of the Dog in the Night-time, The Time Traveller's Wife, We Need to Talk About Kevin* – about all of which they have strong feelings. Two retirement-aged couples are having lunch with wine, while a younger couple are having lunch with beer.

I'm still so stuck in the past that I can't help thinking, 'A cappuccino! In Brookmans Park!' so I text my sister to tell her. When it arrives, the waitress brings me a Lyle's golden syrup tin containing white sugar lumps, and a small china bowl containing nine Smarties. Oh Brookmans Park, I think. Don't ever change. Don't ever get as sophisticated as you think you are. Then I eat the Smarties.

I have a look at the Brookmans newsletter, to bring myself up to date with current concerns. The topics included are: Missing Cat. Trampoline 12 foot. Human excrement in Bulls Lane area. Exploring prayer and healing at Brookmans Park United Reform Church. Two attempted burglaries in The Grove. Spare Lego?

I'd been wondering whether or not modern connectedness, via the internet, might change what it means to grow up in suburbia, making it easier for everyone to experience the same things, at the same time. Maybe today, when kids grow up in a communal, virtual environment, there isn't that same profound sense of detachment, of living far from the centre of things, missing out on what's new and happening? I imagine myself, alone in my bedroom, yet able to connect with other angsty teenage music fans via the internet, even to express myself anonymously, share concerns, access information, and I think how much I would have loved it, how it would have provided a window on to the wider world.

I think of this when people complain about how the internet has made islands of us all, or bemoan the fact that families don't share things any more, each individual member being wedded to a separate screen. So many of the things I share with my kids come to us via the internet, and so I can see how it brings us together just as much as it isolates us. On the rare occasions when we watch telly together, the kids have their phones with them, conducting a Snapchat while viewing. But then, I might be on Twitter too, so who am I to talk? We're the archetypal modern addicted family. It's a cliché, that image of no one talking, everyone locked into a personal screen, and we're supposed to be cross about it, or find it depressing.

But much of the time I find our use of the internet is

sociable, usually based on everyone seeking out jokes, and then sharing the jokes. I've lost count of how many Vines and gifs I've had to peer at on a teenager's phone. Sometimes I get the joke and can honestly LOL, sometimes I don't and they have to explain it to me. But whatever else I shared with parents, I don't remember sharing this many laughs.

And I like the way the sharing goes both ways, the traffic between us moving in both directions. When we gather around my laptop at the end of dinner, so we can all watch the latest Cassetteboy video on YouTube, or clips of Tom Hiddleston dancing on a chat show, or one of them lines up the current Top 10 on a phone for us all to listen to and judge, it feels like the old and the new styles of family life exist side by side. We eat together, we laugh together, we are amazed together. It connects us. So I can only imagine that it would have improved my experience of growing up in suburbia.

Yet here on the newsletter, one of the things being complained about is internet connection, and there is much discussion about the difficulty of cable being laid to the village. Rural broadband access is notoriously bad, a problem that has scuppered many a home-worker's attempt to relocate somewhere scenic, only to confront an endlessly spinning wheel on a screen while trying to work. Yet this is not Cumbria, or the heart of Cornwall – we are only thirty minutes from London here, surely access to the internet should be a given? (Fast-forward to 2017, and a high speed FTTP installation has taken place, although on the newsletter page, debate continues on the topic of village broadband and high-speed optic fibre, still not everyone being covered.)

Good God, I think, perhaps then the experience is even worse. Imagine living in a place that feels physically cut off, and which is also excluded from the non-stop ongoing worldwide conversation taking place online. You'd feel even more uniquely isolated – separate and alone, while out there in the world at large, and just up the road, everyone else was connected, and communicating, and sharing.

A question keeps returning to me though, and it's this – if the suburbs are meant to be a refuge, why aren't they more relaxed? If they're meant to represent safety, why do they teem with anxiety? It's as if the desire for security in itself fosters an increased tendency to worry, a kind of watchful wariness. It's the only way I can explain the sense of fearfulness, the background hum of tension, with which I grew up. That generalised anxiety I shared with Mum now feels inseparable from the place in which we lived, as if all the utopian myths, all the aspirational striving, and the self-sufficiency and the isolation, set up an attitude of distrust towards the world outside, and life in general.

I was a fretful child, afraid of everything, and afraid to say so. I was scared of food, so I walked home every lunchtime, but even the hundred-yard walk from primary school frightened me, and I'd scuttle home as fast as possible. We'd been shown a Public Information film about 'stranger danger' that ended with an abducted girl, cowering against a wall as a dark male shadow loomed over her. I was sure that I'd be kidnapped on my five-minute walk from school, but too panicked to stay and encounter a meal I didn't like.

I'm still the same, and I realise that what separates laid-back people from those like me who are permanently on edge is our response to stimulation. I envy calm people for their apparent immunity to over-excitement or over-reaction. They seem to have a thicker skin than me, impervious to the minor fluctuations of everyday life. It takes something really up tempo to get their hearts racing, so they seek out rollercoasters and fast cars and cocaine – properly adventurous or risky experiences, needing that buzz to feel alive. In contrast, I creep through life on tiptoes, trying not to set off alarms, avoiding stimulants which would tip me over the edge, the inside of my brain and body operating at rollercoaster speed much of the time, even when nothing is happening. My heart races at the slightest provocation, needing no recreational drugs to pump it up, and I'm more likely to get addicted to beta blockers than coke.

Some of my hair fell out when I was about five years old, which was put down to nerves. I developed a twitch, a blinking habit, for which I was teased. I counted the squares on the pavement, having to step on lines with left foot then right, left then right, in an even sequence. I was like a little bird on the bird feeder, forever looking over my shoulder expecting a predator, never settling.

And growing up a girl, these anxieties coalesced around the fear of sexual violence. Then, as now, you were held personally responsible for avoiding attack, and there were rules to be obeyed, clear instructions about how to 'do the right thing', which would keep you safe. There was a footpath that ran alongside the railway line from Brookmans Park to Potters Bar, but I heard tales of women being flashed at or molested. Mum said, 'Don't walk the line path, it's not safe.' There were 'funny men' there. My friend Liz had a story about walking in Peplins Wood with her mum and seeing a man who exposed himself. Without knowing the right words for it, she told me that he was masturbating. There was, she said, 'loads of white stuff pumping out of him'. I pictured it as a torrent, a pulsing flow, like shaving foam, or whipped cream from a canister.

The railway station was slightly apart from the village, isolated down a hill, dark and lonely at night, and walking home alone from the station after dusk was forbidden. Mum said, 'Don't get off the train alone at night,' so my boyfriend would walk me home, and we'd kiss on the railway bridge, and I'd arrive home flustered, lipstick-less, stubble-scratched. But I got the message – even the tiny mile or so of green between us and the next town, even the few steps of darkness from the station, were filled with dangers. As for the fields and woods around us, who knew what might be lurking there.

We'd fled the city only to find that the countryside was equally unsafe. It was hard to know where to turn. The suburb was meant to be a life raft to cling to. But in my teens suburbia developed its own new terrors, when the factionalism of the late '70s meant there were endless fights between rival tribes, skinheads and other thugs, who beat up everyone I knew at some point or other, either at a party, or on the street, or at the 2-Tone gigs at Hatfield

Poly. I wrote about such events in a song called 'Hatfield 1980', specifically about a friend getting stabbed, and it's true that these were aggressive times, but the point is, the suburbs were no safer than the city, perhaps less so, in that you stood out more and were easily picked off by rivals. My parents must have felt at this point that they'd been hoodwinked, and that the suburban dream had not materialised.

Far worse than the scuffles and knife fights I witnessed during my teenage years however, was the fact that in 1986, five years after I'd left the place, and when I was living back in London, and after all the warnings and alarmist scenarios which had been impressed upon me as a teen, a young woman was murdered in Brookmans Park, after dark, beside the railway station. Her name was Anne Lock, and she fell victim to two serial rapists and killers, who were later found guilty of a series of crimes. She was twenty-nine years old and worked for a TV company. She'd just got back from her honeymoon in the Seychelles, when she went to work one day, on May the 18th, leaving her bicycle in the shed at the station. When she got back there late in the evening, it is thought that the two men were waiting for her somewhere in the station car park.

Her body was found two months later, in undergrowth, in a field a little way along the railway track.

Such things can happen anywhere, of course. I think about those theories of dirt being 'matter out of place' explored by anthropologist Mary Douglas in her book *Purity and Danger*. She describes those 'rejected bits and pieces' which are 'recognisably out of place, a threat to good order, and so are regarded as objectionable and vigorously brushed away', and I wonder whether something similar applies to our attitude towards crime. Maybe we're more shocked when violence happens in a place we think it shouldn't. Maybe the lower crime rates of suburbia lull us into a false sense of security, which is nothing more than a daydream; the idea that as long as we lead nice, respectable lives, and are good and obey the rules, we'll be ok. Murder seems out of place in the suburbs and so we simply brush the idea away, reassuring ourselves that danger lurks only in the city, where everyone is rubbing along too close to each other, going out after dark, it's their own fault. But of course it's sheer bad luck, bad timing, to encounter such malevolence, such evil. Suburbia is a risk-averse place to live, its inhabitants hoping that they are somehow magically protected, but it's not true, and dreams of utopia are just that, dreams. Nowhere is immune to tragedy. We always knew that.

1980

I was becoming exhausted by the efforts involved in all this repression. The place briefly turned me into a drama queen. I craved excitement and change. I picked fights, longed for love and looked for trouble. I was restless, intensely passionately solipsistic. Felt utterly trapped and thwarted and beat my wings irritably against the bars of the cage. Everything was pent up inside me, literally it seemed. The night I first told a boy I loved him, my eardrum burst. I was in agony all night with earache, and bleeding by the morning, having suffered a perforation. After I'd seen the doctor and got some penicillin, I went to bed and watched *Cat on a Hot Tin Roof*.

Another night, I went to a party at a girl's house in Harpenden, a '*big house*' I wrote in my diary. It provoked me in some way, stirred up something – Envy? A sense of inadequacy? – and so I dismissed it, rather than think about what this meant, '*v musical evening, everyone playing pianos and guitars all over the place. Rather sedate sort of party though – no recklessness. Dullsville.*' Desperate for something to happen, I kept splitting up with my boyfriend and getting back together two days later, seeking some kind of buzz.

'I told him it was time we had a good argument but he didn't understand. How can I fight him when he always submits?'

We didn't have AS-Levels, so my lower sixth was a layabout year, and with no college websites to look at, I relied on the few prospectuses lying around at school. My parents, as was the norm, left all the choosing and visiting up to me, and were not there to witness my half-hearted mooch around the windswept Hull campus, or my miserable failure of an interview at UEA. I vaguely remember filling in an UCCA form, trying to think of a better reason for wanting to go to a particular university than the hope that they might possibly have me, and then running into real difficulty with the interests and hobbies section.

For despite the fact that my late adolescence was a strange and vivid time to me, it looked bleak and empty when I tried to put it into words. I had no list of achievements to impress an admissions department – I wasn't head girl or a prefect, a Girl Guide or a Duke of Edinburgh award winner. I'd given up piano lessons, didn't play chess, or netball, or any sports at all. Wasn't in the choir or the drama society. My work experience was a paper round and a Saturday job in a toy shop.

Instead, the things that absorbed every second of my waking life were the writing of diaries, and songs, often heartfelt accounts of momentous events involving boys, inspired by my repeated playing of the same few records I owned. As for sport, well I spent a lot of time loitering at bus stops, waiting for a bus, hoping for an idea of somewhere to go. Skulking around the streets of St Albans, we covered lamp posts with stickers for the Marine Girls, the band I'd formed with other girls from school, in a sort of polite, suburban form of graffiti tagging. I recorded some songs and played some gigs, but above all, I dreamed – about the future and the things that might happen. I dreamed and I wondered. When would I find out who I was? Would I be good at anything? Would anyone love me?

None of this was the kind of stuff that worked on a form. Full of doubt, struggling to define myself, I tried to present myself as a fully realised person with relevant interests, clear goals, coherent ambitions. As if any of us are that. The dreaming had led me to books, so I listed all the ones I'd read, some of which had already been chosen to impress an older boy. Camus and Sartre, Zola's *Thérèse Raquin*, Kerouac's *On the Road*. Fine books all, but a slightly erratic combination, more reflective of teenage angst than of the literary canon. They said something about me, but perhaps not what I meant them to.

On February the 9th I stormed out of my job at the supermarket. I'd arrived at work that morning dressed in black trousers, red socks and black pumps, and the new manager said, '*D'you think you could pop home and change into something presentable. Said he'd worked in shops for 5 years and he'd never seen anyone turn up for work looking like that.*' Throwing my overall at him, I stormed out, refusing to ever go back. Meanwhile, my own internal violence was reflected back at me by the aggression we encountered everywhere on the streets.

6 June – On the way home from a gig, '*Saw awful fight – skins/mods – on tube. Really scary. Horrible evening.*'

9 June – '*L went up to the Marquee last night to see the Merton Parkas with a few mod friends and they got beaten up by skins. YUK.'*

But the culmination of my awful behaviour as a girlfriend must be the holiday I went on with Debbie, to Jersey, in July. The day before I left I wrote of The Boyfriend that *'I'll miss him a lot though. This is the longest I've gone without seeing him for ages.'* The next night, in Jersey, I was at a disco dancing with four blokes from Loughborough. The following day, Debbie and I were asked out by two waiters from the hotel, and went with them to a disco called 'Blimpers', followed by a walk along the front. That night I stayed in The Waiter's room. Next evening we went to a disco called the 'Kon Tiki', danced to Dexy's, and I spent the night with The Waiter again. The following day we went to the Lido with the boys from Loughborough, which infuriated The Waiter, so we had a huge row, *'think that's all over now'*. Instead, we went to the *'Skyline disco, where I danced with Terry, then went to the Ritz'*, walked along the beach and got off with Terry. *'Naughty, naughty . . .'*

Next morning we visited the German military hospital, then went to the Skyline disco, and I met a boy called Jerry. By the end of THAT evening, *'I'm in love with Jerry.'* Suddenly it was our last day, I gave my address and phone number to The Waiter, and flew back home to The Boyfriend. *'Feel a bit guilty now about all the fun I've had.'* Well, quite. I had myself become an expert at duplicity. The Waiter phoned me, then a letter arrived from him. *'He misses me a lot and said he's in love with me. In the afternoon he phoned and asked me to go over – I said I had no money and he said he'd send it to me – I said no so he asked me to go on holiday with him – I said no again so eventually he said – Well how about coming over here and getting married! My first proposal. How exciting.'* Dear God, I sound like a Jane Austen character. He phoned a couple more times, then a week later a HUGE bunch of flowers arrived. In my diary I wrote *'I was horrified.'* Mum narrowed her eyes at me. 'What have you been DOING?' She meant, 'Who have you been sleeping with? How far have you been going?'

You'd think all this action would have cheered me up, but no.

10 September – *'I feel in a mood of absolute deep despair.'*

Looking back, it's hard to see exactly what was wrong. I just felt stuck. Some people had gone off to university, and there was a sense of the old gang breaking up. I'd started the Marine Girls by now, but still, there were endless, endless evenings of the same crowd of people sitting in the same few pubs. Without The Boyfriend, *'I went to party in Wormley with Debbie, her Secret Boyfriend and Davina. It was in a marquee in a car park. I got off with a bloke called Alan from Muswell Hill. Gave me his phone number.'* And occasionally The Boyfriend would now do the same to me too, *'Went over to Suzanne's. Boyfriend was supposed to come but he rang about 10 to say he was at Finsbury Park with M and God knows who else, having fun. Little bastard. I hung up on him.'*

On September the 26th I turned eighteen. Finally legal in pubs, after all those forbidden years. *'Got a wonderful*

music centre and Vic Goddard LP and Durutti Column LP.
Music centre = really nice. In the evening we went over to MJ's.
Got drunk and went up the college to see The Tea Set (who were
crap).'

It's supposed to be a milestone, isn't it, turning eighteen? I don't sound like an adult, and I didn't feel like one, and looking back from my now so-very-adult perspective – me in my mid-fifties, a wife, a parent, facing the empty nest myself – I can't quite get to grips with the level of boredom and misery that seemed to engulf me. Would I like to go back there, be eighteen again? And if I could go back in time now, stand face to face with my eighteen-year-old self, what on earth would I say? Who even is that person? I don't think I know her.

Fast-forward thirty-five years and my own daughters would be turning eighteen, a fact which seems no more likely just because I'm looking at it written down. Adults. My babies as adults. It still won't sink in. On their birthday I would keep remembering the Christmas just before they were born, when we cancelled all travel plans in order to be within hospital range, and I stayed at home, struggling through the backache of the day, clutching on to furniture like a drunk, falling asleep in front of *Vertigo*, until finally, each evening I'd lie gratefully in the bath, with the dome of my belly rising above the water like a cartoon desert island.

When New Year came, time sped up, and the problems became an emergency, and the babies arrived six weeks early. Tiny scraps of nothing, each weighing less than four pounds, they lay scrawny and helpless in their incubators, one bright red and the other ghostly white. Curled, gently furred like a leaf. I thought I'd die of love for them. I still think that. For the next few years I'd be queen of their little universe, omniscient, omnipotent, until gradually and so subtly I didn't see it happening, my superpowers slipped away, and they stood level with me, and then began to creep ahead. Until I was full of doubt about the idea of offering words of wisdom or advice to them, so that when they turned eighteen I would simply offer a few thank yous:

'Thanks for all the things you taught me. I taught you to talk, and then you taught me to text. Remember when I got a phone, and for the first year didn't realise people were sending me messages on it? Oh, how we laughed. Oh, how I needed your help. And after that, thanks for teaching me what all the acronyms stand for, and also the latest slang words. (Though I do suspect you make some of them up, and laugh at me for believing you.) And though I taught you the Facts of Life (perhaps), thanks for teaching me the new ones, so that I was ahead of the game that year when everyone starting flinging around non-binary and gender-fluid and I knew what they were talking about.

'Thank you for being brilliant sisters to your younger brother. Remember when he was really little and said indignantly on holiday one year, "God, this song is so SEXIST"? And that day when he came home from school and told me that he had taken issue with one of his mates for saying

"That's so GAY" about something or other. How thrilled we were, and proud of him.

'And above all, even though you're officially adults now, thanks for still being teenagers. I know it's hard, with all the exams and pressure and endless endless STUFF, but nothing makes me happier than seeing your pleasure in being allowed to pierce your ears, or chop your hair off, or dye it peroxide blonde, or pink, or any of the other things I wasn't allowed to do.

'So do I have any advice for you at all? Not really. Except that, like all young people (or come to that, even old people these days), I know you worry sometimes about being cool. But don't. Who cares really? Cool's overrated. Warm is better.'

And I wish someone had said that to me at eighteen, and that I might have believed them.

I realise of course, that much of the time I was just being a cliché, and that it is very much teenagers who hate suburbia, which is why there are so many pop song lyrics about it. It's for squares, for drones, worst of all, for PARENTS, who love it for the quality of life it offers. Young people don't care about such things as comfort and cleanliness – they want culture, and night life, and energy.

There are no clubs or pavement cafés in suburbia. You can't explore it at night, as – say – Dickens walked the streets of London. Who walks around suburbia at night? It would be spooky and weird. You can't be a suburban *flâneur*. Suburbia is for those who want a quiet life, with no alarms and no surprises. It goes to bed early, and after dark, when a teenager comes alive, the streets are silent.

Over and over again, you find examples of teenage disdain for all this. Hanif Kureishi (another product of Bromley) captures this in *The Buddha of Suburbia*, where teenage Karim is suitably sarcastic: 'In the suburbs people rarely dreamed of striking out for happiness. It was all familiarity and endurance: security and safety were the reward of dullness.' Like many such teens, he can't understand why his parents have inflicted this life on him: 'I often wondered why he'd condemned his own son to a dreary suburb of London of which it was said that when people drowned they saw not their lives but their double-glazing flashing before them.'

Children often enjoy what suburbia has to offer – I think back to my own happy childhood here – so perhaps the teenager is rejecting not just parents, but childhood. It seems like a marker of growing up to start hating it, to feel that the place itself is childish, that its cosiness has an infantilising effect. Teenagers rage at suburbia, which equals their parents, screaming, 'You don't UNDERSTAND me! You never let me do ANYTHING! Stop babying me! You're so square! I HATE you!'

In song lyrics of the '60s and '70s, there's a high-minded, anti-materialistic strand to the objections. In The Monkees' 'Pleasant Valley Sunday', suburbia is simply 'status symbol land', built on ideals that are meaningless to the young – 'And the kids just don't understand / Creature comfort goals, they only numb my soul'. There's often a sense that suburbia is an emasculated environment, maybe because it represents a life entirely domesticated, and set up for the needs of the family. In 'Semi-detached Suburban Mr James' by Manfred Mann, there are lots of lyrics like, 'Do you think you will be happy, buttering the toast' and 'So you think you will be happy, taking doggie for a walk'. The song is aimed at a woman who has scorned the writer to marry someone else, dooming herself to a sexless life of routine and drudgery: 'I can see you in the morning time / Washing day, the weather's fine / Hanging things upon the line / And as your life slips away . . .' What it comes down to is that the new suburban lover 'can't love you the way I can, so please don't you forget it', which makes me think there is often something more going on than just liberal rejection of convention, and that what might have felt like sticking it to 'The Man', was actually, more often than not, a case of sticking it to the woman. A woman who might have been a stand-in for the writer's mum.

Suburbia – so cosy, so domestic – is a feminised place, and this seems to be the source of some of rock's scorn and contempt. Again, in 'Pleasant Valley Sunday', the women are apparently blind to how comfy and privileged their lives are, actually having the audacity to find life looking after a teenager quite difficult: 'Mothers complain about how hard life is.' The teenager, of course, being far too evolved to get any pleasure from the creature comforts that numb his soul.

In other songs, the plight of suburban woman is explicitly recognised. 'The Ballad of Lucy Jordan', written by Shel Silverstein in the mid-'70s, takes place 'In a white suburban bedroom / In a white suburban town', where Lucy comes to the realisation that 'she'd never ride / Through Paris in a sports car / With the warm wind in her hair', and is instead doomed to 'clean the house for hours', until she either cracks up or commits suicide, depending on how you read the ending of the song. By 1978, in 'Suburban Relapse' by Siouxsie and the Banshees, which I listened to endlessly in my bedroom, the breakdown had become explicit:

I'm sorry that I hit you
But my string snapped
I'm sorry I disturbed your cat-nap
But whilst finishing a chore
I asked myself 'what for'
Then something snapped
I had a relapse . . . A Suburban relapse.

I was washing up the dishes
Minding my own business
When my string snapped
I had a relapse . . . A Suburban relapse.

This is definitely a woman speaking, a housewife and mother by the sound of it, at the end of her tether. Siouxsie, part of the Bromley punk contingent, grew up in Chislehurst and the rejection of the suburban housewife role was strong in her. We'd grown up, partly watching our mothers swallowed up by what looked to us like stultifying lives, and partly seeing negative examples of such women on the telly. In dramas and sitcoms, the suburban housewife was sex-starved and frustrated, or desperately aspirational and bullying towards the hen-pecked menfolk. Thelma in *The Likely Lads* was always trying to better herself and spoil the fun, Margo in *The Good Life* was humourless and snobbish. Yootha Joyce's character in *George and Mildred*, a sitcom about a couple who left their council flat for a more upmarket housing estate, much to the dismay of their toffee-nosed neighbour, was also trying to climb the social ladder, but was constantly thwarted by George, who was lazy and feckless.

Beverley in Mike Leigh's *Abigail's Party* was the epitome of this suburban nightmare housewife – lacking in culture, self-awareness or tact, she was socially crass and yet seething with a thwarted energy, spitting at her husband that 'Just because a picture happens to be erotic, does not make it pornographic.' Lusting after Demis Roussos, desperate for something, ANYTHING to happen, she was mocked by the play, but Alison Steadman's performance is what everyone remembers, it was her energy and pent-up urges that drove the piece along. Even at the time, some people could see that there was something sneering about this portrayal – Dennis Potter wrote of the play that it was 'a prolonged jeer, twitching with genuine hatred, about the dreadful suburban tastes of the dreadful lower-middle classes'.

But all these showed us a type of behaviour for which women were particularly disliked. It was the women who were to blame, seemingly – leading the men astray, emasculating them, curtailing their natural freedoms, forcing them into domesticity and acquisitiveness. No wonder as teenagers we were so afraid of ending up like that, of turning into our mothers. No wonder we looked at suburbia and wanted to burn it down.

1981

Eighteen years old. A Collins, black pocket diary, page to a day. There are no phone numbers tucked inside, but instead a long quote from Kerouac's *On the Road*: 'the evening star must be drooping and shedding her sparkler dims on the prairie, which is just before the coming of complete night that blesses the earth, darkens all rivers, cups the peaks and folds the final shore in, and nobody, nobody knows what's going to happen to anybody besides the forlorn rags of growing old'. I still love that line, the forlorn rags of growing old.

There are also quotes from 'Every Time We Say Goodbye', 'Until the Real Thing Comes Along', 'My Man' and 'I Cover the Waterfront', all down to my Billie Holiday obsession. And written on the inside back page, a list of my all-time favourite films – *Badlands, Manhattan, The Misfits* and *The Graduate . . . Annie Hall, Love and Death, Being There, Gaslight* and *Camille . . . Paths to Glory, All Quiet on the Western Front, It Always Rains on Sundays* and *Casablanca . . . Women in Love, Cabaret, Brief Encounter, Gregory's Girl* and *A Matter of Life and Death*. If I made a list today it wouldn't be much different, which makes me think, have I changed at all since that year? And had I seen all the films I would ever love by the age of nineteen?

As the year began, I finally completely split up with The Boyfriend, and declared '*I'm in love with Orange Juice!*' And the diary starts with a declaration:

1 January – '*New year marks a definite attempt to make this diary a bit more interesting. Less trivia etc.*'

Of course in retrospect, it's the trivia that's interesting, and not all the declarations of despair and boredom, but this is the eighteen-year-old me speaking. I was aware that it was becoming repetitive. What the resolution meant, though, was that I did actually start trying to talk about my feelings. At a party, I had a long, deep discussion with a boy: '*We talked about how we both used to act being cynical but really we're both hopeful about life. It really was a good conversation.*' This might have been the first time I used an encounter with a boy at a party to have a conversation.

My diary entries in general reveal less drama, but a sort of undercurrent of yearning, for love and for maturity.

26 February – '*Heard "Ceremony" by New Order. Best thing I've heard in ages. It's wonderful. A favourite single of all time already.*'

6 April – '*I've taken up yoga.*'

16 April – '*The Cure were on* Top of the Pops. *I'm in love with Robert Smith.*'

My A-Levels began on Tuesday, June the 2nd, with a history exam described in my diary as *'about as bad as expected'*. But the run up to this had hardly seen me sweating non-stop over a textbook. I'd spent the Saturday night at the Moonlight Club in West Hampstead, where I *'saw a really good band called Maximum Joy, and Pigbag, who were wonderful. Danced my legs off.'* On the Sunday, instead of fretting about the upcoming exam, I was wondering whether we ought to record a single. Finally, on the day before A-Levels started, I did some *'last minute work'*, although to balance that, in the evening I *'saw an Elizabeth Taylor film,* Butterfield 8'.

So maybe it was no surprise the first exam didn't go brilliantly. I went to another gig that night, to see a local band featuring *'2 guitars, bass, vocals and bongos. Brilliant.'* Then another one on the Friday. A brief moment of studiousness kicked in on Wednesday, June the 3rd, when I actually turned a gig down – *'Mark, TV Personalities drummer, phoned to say he got us a gig at the Moonlight club on June 18th. Day before my English exam, can't really do it. Damnation.'*

The following Monday, June the 8th, was my first economics exam, which was apparently *'ok'*, but more importantly we got confirmation from Rough Trade that they wanted fifty copies of our cassette. Next day I had a Shakespeare paper, which was *'appalling'*, followed two days later by a history exam – *'pretty foul'* – although this was leavened by the news that Rough Trade were going to send twenty-five copies of our cassette to America. *'They said they love us!'*

Saturday night I went to a party, where I got off with a boy who '*likes jazz, blues and Paris, and sings in a band*', then had an English exam on the Monday, and bought 'Back to My Roots' by Odyssey. Tuesday was my final economics paper, about which I tersely record '*no comment*'. On Friday, June the 19th I sat my Chaucer paper, and with a nonchalant '*A LEVELS OVER*' I headed up to London to sell some tapes to Rough Trade. Friday, June the 26th was my official school leaving day. The night before I'd been at the Lyceum to see *The Birthday Party*, supported by Vic Godard and Subway Sect. At school I '*got £4 book token prize for English and History*'. Later the same day Gina from the Marine Girls rang, '*and read me a review of* Beach Party *– really over the top. Said I had a voice with a future – rich, controlled and soulful! hahaha.*'

That 'hahaha' says it all. In retrospect, all this looks like the beginning of a career, the opening scenes of a biopic even, but in truth I wasn't taking music seriously, in the sense of worrying about whether I had a voice with a future, and nor was I taking school seriously, in the sense of worrying about my academic future. I was living entirely in the moment, caught up in the whirl of exciting things like gigs and music, skating across the surface of boring things like school. My results came in:

15 August – '*I got A for English, C for history, E for economics. Will it be good enough . . .?*' It was a bit late to start wondering.

'Life goes on tediously, nothing happens for months, and then one day everything, and I mean everything, goes fucking wild and berserk.'
— Hanif Kureishi, *The Buddha of Suburbia*

Things didn't quite go berserk for me, but they changed, and changed utterly, from the day I left home, on October the 3rd.

I went up to Hull, and Mum and Dad took off for Canada, taking the train across the Rockies, and finally visiting the wild brave relations who had moved there all those years ago, and who now, according to Mum, lived up a mountain, with their five children and countless grand-children, in a real life version of *The Waltons*. As far from suburbia as could be, their life was wide open, full of the great outdoors, expansive and rugged. Photos of my parents on the ranch show Mum in a stetson, and Dad with a holster belted around his hips, carrying a rifle. They were transported up and down the steep track in a truck which they feared had no brakes, driven round hairpin bends at breakneck speed, by strapping young Canadians who were somehow our flesh and blood, though as far removed from us as could be imagined.

When they got back home to Brookmans Park, Mum learned to drive, and though she never went any further than the golf club, or occasionally to Welwyn Garden City, it must have represented some attempt on her part to re-invent herself, to try something new. Meanwhile I met Ben, and then moved in with him, and my parents' tolerance for something new was stretched to the limit and then broke, their judgement falling on me like icy rain. Because of the falling out which ensued, I never properly went back home to live in the suburbs. I spent a couple of weeks there over the first Christmas, but by the following summer I was completely gone and would never return. They must have cleared out my room at some point, and thrown away lots of stuff, without ever checking with me. God knows what they would have found in the back of my cupboards. They never said. For a while we weren't saying a lot to each other. I'd spent much of my teens wanting to break free and shake them off, but when the breach came it shook me in a way I hadn't anticipated and didn't even recognise for what it was at the time.

Up at Hull University, living with Ben and feeling the cold chill of disapproval from home, I had something of a mini-breakdown. Panic attacks, anxiety, an overwhelming sense of dread that settled on me from the moment I woke in the morning and followed me like a cloud from lecture to seminar to library and then back home again, where I'd cry for no reason and have nightmares about giant spiders falling on me from the ceiling. True to form I dealt with this by not mentioning it, suppressing everything, at least in conversation. Although maybe it DID come out, in the songs I wrote, or the tone of my singing. Something about that undercurrent of melancholy, that very obvious vulnerability, sounds to me now like a cry for help, or an articulation of emotions I couldn't put into words. I didn't understand until many years later, that I had probably been depressed during this period, and that the achieving of my independence – which I had longed for – came at great personal cost.

In the early '90s my parents finally left Brookmans Park, but it was a huge wrench for Mum, and the thinking about leaving went on forever, too long for Dad. I sat in the car with him one day, getting a lift back to somewhere, and he was at his wit's end. 'We keep going to look at houses, and one minute she likes one, and then the next day she's changed her mind again.' They thought about relocating to the seaside, a change of lifestyle for their retirement, but for Mum, leaving the home where we'd all grown up was terrifying, marking as it did the complete end of that part of her life. Eventually they moved to be near Debbie, on a new-build estate on the outskirts of Newbury, into – Oh joy of joys! – a detached house.

Mum was thrilled. There were extra bedrooms upstairs, for grandchildren to sleep in, and though they rarely did and mostly just needed extra hoovering, her pleasure in the house was undiminished. It was the prize, finally won, after all the suburban dreaming.

But the distance that had grown up between me and

my parents in my teens never quite closed up, and it was due in part to my increased education and change of lifestyle. Like so many similar parents, they'd wanted me to do well at school and then go to university, to take those chances they'd never had. Then when I did, it turned me into someone they thought they couldn't understand. Later on they'd be proud of my musical success, but perhaps more because it was success, and therefore respectable, than because it was artistically interesting to them. They liked the music when it was more mainstream, and they liked the gigs at the Albert Hall because they were tangible proof of achievement and status, and they enjoyed the sense of pride and reflected glory at the backstage party, and all of this was soothing and reassuring to them because it took away some of the fear that they had lost me to rock and roll.

As Ben has written, we never know our parents as we are growing up, only getting to understand them once we are ourselves standing in their old, discarded shoes, and perhaps it can't be any other way. You hear people talk about 'the family drama', and if there is such a thing then it often feels like the characters in it are sketchily drawn and two-dimensional. And the role of parent, which seems so demanding while you're playing it, requires mostly that you under-act. That you don't commandeer too much of the spotlight, or step out of character, or ad-lib, or ask what your motivation is. But if we don't know our parents, I do also wonder whether they ever know us.

In later years, after my break to have children, when I went back to music and recorded an album called *Out of the Woods* in 2007, I sent them a copy, expecting a phone call or something a day or two later. Hoping for parental praise, as you always do, as you still do even when you're a grown-up and a success and a mother. It never came. They never mentioned it, or said anything about the record. Debbie told me later they'd found it hard to understand, and I was never sure what exactly was hard to understand. The music? Or the reason for making a record? The need? Perhaps that.

Later still, when I wrote *Bedsit Disco Queen*, my dad's only comment to Debbie was, 'I never knew Tracey was so into music.' Which still makes me laugh till I cry for all it says about how much we can remain a complete and utter mystery to those who should know us the best.

And then again, in even later years, he would say to Debbie, in reference to something or other I had done, some inexplicable action, some bizarre life choice – and this, remember, when I was a middle-aged, middle-class woman, married to the man I'd been with for over thirty years, with three children, living a respectable middle-class life in a respectable middle-class enclave of north London – he would say, 'Oh, Tracey. She's from another planet.'

Another planet.

2016

> This is the place I live
> Where is everyone? Are we the only ones?
> This is the place I live
> And so does everyone, and so does everyone
>
> (Hatfield, 1980)

After that I start to walk up Brookmans Avenue, past the bigger detached houses, away from the village, and into the posh bit of Brookmans Park, where Mum always longed to live. Some houses have been rebuilt in more modern style, the faux Tudorbethan replaced by granite and steel, prison-like edifices. 2009 is carved into the stone of one, and there's a building site where another is being rebuilt, just a gaping hole for the foundations. And then I notice that there's no proper pavement up here. Lawns run right down to the road, and are broken up by gravel and pebbles that extend out from driveways. It would be a nightmare to negotiate with a pushchair or wheelchair, and even as a pedestrian it feels awkward and unwelcoming. You are meant to be in your car. There is no path for you. Why are you here? Who are you and where are you going?

It is silent up at the top end of the village, apart from birdsong. The playing fields of Chancellor's School look idyllic in the spring sunshine – kids playing football, lounging about. But this far from the shops, and from where I grew up, I feel less at home, stranded in the smart bit. I realise how different the two sides of town are, though town is the wrong word. How can such a small, homogenous village have such a clear sense of a wrong and right side of the tracks? And I am struck with the feeling that where we lived, in the bustle of the village, was actually the best bit. From our house you could hear the primary school playground, and we were near enough to watch the fireworks on Bonfire Night from our bedroom window. The houses are smaller and closer together, but there's a sense of community. Up at the top end it is more exclusive, but quieter, creepier and deader. Apart from me, there is hardly anyone around, just the occasional car passing. There are builders up on scaffolding working on refurbishments. A man in a blue shirt with a white collar gets out of his Range Rover on his gravel drive. Two teenagers pass me going towards the school, one an unhappy-looking boy with glasses and a man-bun.

There's something claustrophobic about the smallness of these suburban roads, you can't even call them streets, with their low-rise buildings and half-size trees, something cramped and Toytown, which contrasts with the grandeur you can find in both rural and urban scenery. I sit at the top of our house, here at the top of a hill in north London, and look out over a wide spreading landscape, full of buildings, but with highs and lows, peaks and troughs, towers, blocks, cranes, a skyline like a mountain range or a series of cliffs and away in the distance, the hills out beyond the south-west of London. And yet the suburban smallness bred in me a fear of true wildness, a dislike of extreme landscape. I'm not comfortable in actual mountains, or near the edges of actual cliffs, or too far out at sea. I don't like isolation, or distance from other people. I need lights dotted across the hills at night, others nearby to call on for help.

My family were rural, then urban, and then suburban, a pattern repeated in countless other families, and reflecting the changes that have taken place in the way most people live. But my ancestors left me a trail of breadcrumbs through the woods that led me back to London, where I have always had a greater sense of freedom, taken a greater breath of fresh air. When I travel back into town, I relax at the first sight of Trellick Tower, or Centrepoint, or St Pancras, but today a different part of me relaxed at the sight of the village green and the low-rise, fake-Tudor-beamed shops and the bungalows and the front gardens.

And for all my musical melancholy, the slightly laconic miserabilism of some of my lyrics, I have also inherited an awful lot of Can-Do cheerfulness from my parents. When our youngest had his thirteenth birthday, I got a wonderful text from my dad saying, 'All I remember about turning thirteen is being allowed to smoke in the bomb shelter.' It made me laugh out loud, but then I suddenly stopped, and for the first time ever pictured my dad, a thirteen-year-old little man, huddled in some underground bunker in Finsbury Park sucking on a fag, while planes flew overhead trying to kill him. My heart turned over a bit, with empathy and guilt, as I imagined anyone trying to do that to MY thirteen-year-old little man, and recognised how blasé I had always been about the things that happened to both my dad and my mum.

I'd grown up hearing their war stories without ever finding them very frightening, or shocking, or real. They simply were. The war was long over, and – far from growing up in its dark shadow – I lived with a cosy version of it, played out via *Dad's Army*, and my brother's Airfix models of Spitfires, and the boys in the playground shouting, 'You be the Nazis,' as an alternative to 'You be the Indians.' And my parents were of that generation brought up to make light of things and put on a brave face, so they made little effort to convey to us the terror hidden in their anecdotes. Wary of frightening us, they made their adventures sound funny and exciting. So Mum told us, 'I was a bit of a bolshy teenager and one night I was just too stroppy to go down into the shelter, so I stayed in my bed, and as I lay there a bomb fell and I watched as my bedroom wall split open in front of my eyes so I could see the street outside.' While Dad said, 'My brother and I had to share a bed and this bomb dropped so close that Tony was blown clean out of bed and across the room, HAHAHA.' It was all as real to me as an Ealing comedy, and no more alarming.

They were an irrepressible generation, at least on the surface, and while that burying of trouble caused them as much, if not more, trouble than it saved them, it also brought with it a kind of resilience, a refusal to be defeated. A sense of obligation towards keeping one's own, and other people's pecker up, which can be socially supportive and sustaining. And so I feel like I'm breaking the code completely and utterly by talking about myself so much here (and I can only do it, in all honesty, now they are both gone).

I walk back down the hill to the station, head over to the platform to wait for my train, and I think about homesickness and what it means. In their book *Edgelands*, Paul Farley and Michael Symmons Roberts talk about the idea that humans have a kind of longing for a return to nature. 'Welsh poets use the word "hiraeth", which describes an anguished sense of separation from home ground, from the land you know and love. It is much deeper than "homesickness", but it is a kind of sickness. And the only cure, we're told, is to go back. Back home, back to the forests and mountains, press your nose to the ground and know that this is where you came from.'

But what if you didn't come from forests and mountains? What if you'd have to press your nose to the crazy paving of the driveway to know that this is where you came from? What does it mean to feel that homesickness for suburbia? Because the truth is, I do feel it. So many of us live in some version of suburbia, the majority of us I suspect, yet we heap scorn upon the place, and what does that do, I wonder, to our sense of self. My relationship with Brookmans Park is complicated, and always will be. I feel terribly at home here, and terribly out of place.

At the end of this day trip into the past, I sit down on the station platform bench and think about my suburban bones. A stream of memory running like a film in my head. I once met a boy on this very platform, dressed in a drape jacket and brothel creepers, and he looked Italian or Middle Eastern and told me his name was Akis. We flirted, and I wondered where he'd come from, and I made up a whole scenario about him in my head but never saw him again. The minutes tick by and four fast trains hurtle through, one heading north, three on their way to London. 'The next train will not be stopping, please stand back from the platform edge.' I've sat here so many times, thought so many thoughts. The trains used to have separate compartments and tweed seat covers, and you'd get a ticket made of thick cardboard. To Potters Bar, or to Welwyn Garden City, or better still, to Highbury & Islington. I wasn't allowed to come here after dark, and I never did. I dreamed of leaving and doubted if I ever would. No, that's not true, I knew I would. At the age of eighteen when I went to Paris, I packed a suitcase full of books, which I then had to haul one step at a time up over the footbridge, Mum laughing at me and asking, 'What on EARTH have you got in there?' Everything was a ticket out of here, everything was a possibility; the days couldn't come fast enough. Now I have all the time in the world, and I'm waiting for a slower, stopping train. From the bench I am looking directly at the car park and I wonder, does anyone remember what happened there? Are commuters haunted by it, or has it faded into the distant past? A schoolgirl comes down the steps to the platform and she's got headphones on and she's laughing at her phone and she doesn't notice me at all. A phone would have made life difficult for me, I think. All those lies about missed coaches and broken phone boxes. It would have been even harder to live my double life. It would have thwarted my secrets and lies. I look up and the girl has vanished, perhaps I imagined her? Was she some ghost version of me? Did I summon her up out of an alternate universe where I lived here forever and nothing ever happened and the bus never came and the phone never rang and the library was shut and I couldn't get a jumper or a skirt?

When the slow train finally arrives, no one except me gets on or off. I look back once over my shoulder before I step on. And the doors close behind me.

AUTHOR'S NOTE

This book started life as a long essay called 'Green Belt', which told the story of my growing up in suburban England. Over time, the essay began to grow, swallowing up some other recent pieces of writing – reviews, and articles, and columns. These writings were mostly reflections on the things that helped me escape from the confines of 1970s suburbia – music, and art, and time. What this means is that a few short sections of *Another Planet* have appeared previously (in the *New Statesman*, the *Spectator*, on Radio Three and in a Virago collection), although here they are chopped up, rearranged, in some cases rewritten, and take their place within the story as it unfolds.

The North Mymms History Project website was a valuable source of local information, particularly the following: *A Modern History of Brookmans Park 1700–1950* by Peter Kingsford, *A History of Brookmans Park Transmitting Station* by Lilian Caras, *Brookmans Park: Population and Housing* by Richard Potter.

ACKNOWLEDGEMENTS

Thanks to my sister Debbie, and my brother Keith, for letting me write about the place and family we share.

Thanks to my agent Kirsty McLachlan, for being the first to read this as a work in progress, and for seeing potential in the idea.

Thanks to Francis Bickmore at Canongate, for being open-minded about what a book can be, for believing in my writing and being ambitious on my behalf.

Thanks to Octavia Reeve and Vicki Rutherford for attention to detail.

Thanks to Kate Mossman and Tom Gatti at the New Statesman, for things I've learned about editing.

Thanks to Ben for support and encouragement and love.

And thanks to Alfie and Jean and Blake, for being great.

PERMISSION CREDITS

Every effort has been made to trace copyright holders and obtain their permission for the use of copyright material. The publisher apologises for any errors or omissions and would be grateful if notified of any corrections that should be incorporated in future reprints or editions of this book.

Excerpt from 'Bittersweet', Words and Music by Tracey Thorn © 1985 Cherry Red Music Ltd. Complete Music Ltd. All Rights Reserved. International Copyright Secured. Used by permission of Hal Leonard Europe Limited.

Excerpt from 'Come On Home', Words and Music by Ben Watt and Tracey Thorn © 1986. Reproduced by permission of Sony/ATV Music Publishing (UK) Ltd, London W1F 9LD.

Excerpt from 'Frost And Fire', Words and Music by Ben Watt and Tracey Thorn © 1985 Cherry Red Music Ltd. Complete Music Ltd. All Rights Reserved. International Copyright Secured. Used by permission of Hal Leonard Europe Limited.